DEADLY DUOS

DEADLY DUOS

Partners in Crime and their Addiction to Murder

PAUL ROLAND

ARCTURUS

ARCTURUS

This edition published in 2010 by Arcturus Publishing Limited
26/27 Bickels Yard, 151–153 Bermondsey Street,
London SE1 3HA

Copyright © 2010 Arcturus Publishing Limited

ISBN: 978-1-84837-623-6
AD001218EN

Printed in Singapore

CONTENTS

'WE ALL GO A LITTLE MAD SOMETIMES'

NORMAN BATES

Norman Bates, the schizophrenic serial killer in Robert Bloch's novel *Psycho* – and Alfred Hitchcock's cinematic shocker of the same name – expressed a fear that haunts us all: namely, the nagging suspicion that even the most well-balanced person might be capable of murder if pushed too far.

Fortunately, most of us will never know what destructive potential we possess, but in the following pages you will meet numerous individuals who have committed multiple murders and subjected their victims to unimaginable suffering, and yet have expressed no regrets or remorse. The sensation-seeking media call such people 'evil' and demonize them as 'monsters' in a desperate effort to distance them from law-abiding members of society.

But the unpalatable truth is that sexual predators, serial killers and sadists are deceptively ordinary people – on the surface at least. They are not clinically insane, although it would be easier for us to 'understand' their aberrant behaviour if they were. A person of unsound mind will act irrationally and will disregard the risks of getting caught when committing a criminal act. But even the most depraved sex offenders exercise some degree of control over their desires, selecting their victims because of their vulnerability rather than their physical attractiveness. Such people do not act on impulse, even though they often claim that they are overcome by their desires when they see a potential victim. They will have brooded on their crime for days, weeks or even months. But at some point they realize that their fantasy no longer satisfies them, so they take the opportunity to make it a reality. All multiple murderers and serial sex killers are predators and they hunt using their intellect as much as their instincts.

Sadistic serial killers are frequently well organized and well prepared. Many of them use a customized vehicle for the abduction of their victims and they often have a secluded base where they can hold them for as long as they serve their purpose. These are not the actions of an insane person. Even the most depraved killers will attempt to evade detection, which proves that they are capable of reasoning and are therefore legally responsible for their actions.

To divert suspicion they might cultivate an air of respectability by leading an ordered life and holding down a regular job, which is not the act of a person of unsound mind. Such offenders are abnormal, not insane.

It also needs to be acknowledged that sexual desire is not always the motive behind the crimes of serial sex offenders and sadistic killers. In many cases rape and torture are expressions of deep-seated anger. These disturbed individuals have a need to manipulate, dominate and control their victims.

But are these people born evil or has cruelty been instilled in them at an impressionable age? The prevailing theory is that many serious offenders were desensitized to suffering through years of abuse and neglect in their childhood. But while other abuse victims internalize their anguish, sexual predators, sadists or serial killers will externalize it. They derive pleasure from watching others suffer as they did and they get a kick out of being in control. The threat to society is doubled when an aggressive psychotic teams up with a passive-aggressive individual who has internalized their anger. This suppressed rage then finds an outlet when their evil twin reinforces their warped view of the world.

When I began researching the cases examined in this book I was a staunch opponent of capital punishment, an advocate of depriving such offenders of their liberty but not their lives. Let them be forced to face the fact that they and they alone are responsible for their incarceration and maybe, just maybe, their conscience might torture them so they suffer even a thousandth of the pain they caused their victims, their families and their friends.

However, the deeper I peered into this abyss, the more disheartened I became. I could see how easily and cynically these heartless individuals had manipulated the justice system, prolonging the agony of the surviving victims and their grieving families. It is a disheartening fact that these criminals simply do not understand that what they have done is abhorrent to every right-minded person. They continue to see themselves as the victims of a society that does not share their psychosis and they have become adept at playing to the media, which feeds their insatiable hunger for recognition and notoriety.

I am reminded of the opinion of a clinical psychiatrist, who dismissed the idea that violent antisocial offenders could be rehabilitated by declaring that the act of educating a psychopath will only produce an educated psychopath.

You may, of course, choose to differ.

Paul Roland

CHAPTER 1

DARK TALES FROM THE BLACK MUSEUM

We have been conditioned to view the past as being full of larger-than-life criminals such as Sweeney Todd and Jack The Ripper. But such 'colourful' characters were comparatively rare and psychotic partnerships were practically unheard of. Perhaps that is why Burke and Hare, Bonnie and Clyde, The Honeymoon Killers and Gordon and Sarah Northcott linger in our collective consciousness like a bad dream.

FRESH CORPSES FOR SALE –
BURKE AND HARE

'UP THE CLOSE AND DOWN THE STAIR,
IN THE HOUSE WITH BURKE AND HARE,
BURKE'S THE BUTCHER, HARE'S THE THIEF,
KNOX THE BOY THAT BUYS THE BEEF.'

SCOTTISH CHILDREN'S RHYME (ANON)

In early 19th century Edinburgh even the dead did not rest easy. No sooner were corpses interred in the city's cemeteries than they were likely to be dug up in the dead of night by 'resurrectionists' – grave robbers who profited from selling cadavers to the local medical schools.

The golden age of scientific discovery was dawning and the Scottish capital's surgeons were keen to supply their eager students with suitable specimens. However, they were forbidden to do so by an antiquated law which supported the Church's assertion that the act of dissection condemned the soul of the deceased to eternal damnation. It was said that only those whose bodies were intact would enter the kingdom of heaven on the Day of Judgment. As a consequence anatomists were forced to limit their examinations to the corpses of executed criminals and vagrants.

Contrary to popular belief, comparatively few criminals were executed at the turn of the century. Instead, transportation to the colonies had become the preferred punishment for all crimes apart from treason and murder, so fresh specimens from the scaffold were in short supply. Consequently, the only question asked of those selling cadavers was, 'Can you obtain another?' And if so, the fresher the better.

Burke (left) had a chip on his shoulder about finding work, while Hare was always looking for get-rich-quick schemes

As the grisly trade increased, grieving relatives were forced to consider paying for the installation of 'mort safes' – iron, cage-like contraptions built over and around the graves of the newly deceased, for fear they might be disinterred at dead of night. But few could afford such measures.

While the more enlightened medical men lobbied unsuccessfully for a change in the law, two of their fellow citizens forced the issue by murdering at least 17 people, often their neighbours, in order to procure fresh cadavers. Ironically, neither of Britain's most notorious bodysnatchers personally robbed a grave during their brief criminal careers. They were either too frightened or too workshy to dirty their hands in the kirkyard.

At the time of the murders, which took place between November 1827 and October of the following year, itinerant Irish immigrant William Burke was 36 years old. He considered himself ill-used by society, with no prospect of finding gainful employment and no will to look for it. After abandoning his wife and two children in County Mayo, he emigrated to Scotland where he drifted aimlessly through a succession of labouring jobs. He ended up in Edinburgh where he settled down with Helen (Nell) McDougal, whom he had met while lodging at her home in Maddiston. Helen left her two children and her common law husband

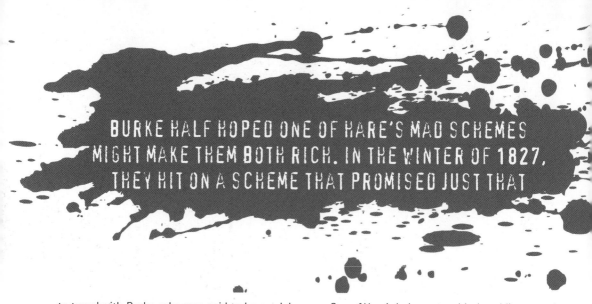

BURKE HALF HOPED ONE OF HARE'S MAD SCHEMES MIGHT MAKE THEM BOTH RICH. IN THE WINTER OF 1827, THEY HIT ON A SCHEME THAT PROMISED JUST THAT

to travel with Burke, who was said to be crudely handsome but sullen and quick-tempered. The couple found cheap lodgings in Tanner's Close in the West Port, a rat run of squalid tenements, gaslit streets and ale houses, where the inhabitants could drink themselves senseless for a shilling.

A FRIGHTFUL SCHEME

With no work, and no hope of finding any, Burke reluctantly endured the company of his landlord, fellow Irish immigrant William Hare, who was generous with his rental income. Hare would buy drinks for anyone who would listen to his idle boasts and his plans to get rich without doing a day's honest work. Little is known of Hare's background, but according to contemporary accounts he was a repulsive, vindictive man who was given to fits of idiotic laughter, when his reptilian features would distort into a hideous mask, giving the impression of a fairground freak. Burke tolerated him so long as he bought the drinks, but he also half hoped that one of Hare's mad schemes might one day make them both rich. In the winter of 1827 they hit on a scheme that promised to do just that.

One of Hare's lodgers, an elderly soldier named Donald, had died suddenly after a long illness. While waiting for the body to be collected, Hare complained long and bitterly to Burke. The old man's rent remained unpaid and there were no known relatives that could be badgered into settling the account. Then it occurred to him that the medical colleges would pay for the corpse, perhaps even more than he was owed. They would split the money equally and be rich men by nightfall. No one would miss the old man or enquire into the cause of his death and there was no risk of being caught – but they would have to act quickly. So they swiftly removed the body from its coffin, hid it elsewhere in the house and replaced it with firewood. After the coffin had been collected they went in search of Professor Munro, the principal anatomist at Edinburgh University Medical School, but by chance they were misdirected to the classrooms of Professor Robert Knox, his colleague. Knox's assistants assured them that they would receive a good price and they were asked to return after dark. When they did so, carrying the still-warm corpse in a sack, Knox's

In the days before refrigeration, murder was more lucrative than 'bodysnatching' since a fresh corpse earned top dollar

assistants gave them just over £7, more than two weeks' wages for the average skilled labourer.

MERCY KILLINGS

Any fears the two Irishmen might have had were soon dissolved by the keg of whisky they consumed that night. Emboldened by their success and excited by the prospect of more easy money, they were soon looking for their next subject. They did not have long to wait.

A few days later another of Hare's lodgers, Joseph the Miller, fell ill. Although his condition was clearly not life-threatening, Burke and Hare saw no necessity in prolonging the man's agony. They plied him with whisky until he lost consciousness, then one of them pinned his arms and legs down while the other covered his nose and mouth until all signs of life were extinct. Unwittingly, the pair had invented a new method of murder, one which would be named after its creator – 'burking'. It was crude, cruel but foolproof because it left no marks on the body. At first glance it appeared that the victim had died of drink or natural causes.

If Burke and Hare had been careful they could have continued enriching themselves in this way for years. But they drank the wages of sin as soon as they collected them and they also became impatient. They no longer wanted to wait for another ailing lodger to come their way. Instead, they went in search of their victims – those who no one would miss, such as tinkers wandering the cobbled streets and drunks sleeping in doorways.

During the following 11 months Burke and Hare committed 15 more murders without arousing suspicion. Their victims included prostitutes, beggars and the homeless. Many of them had come down to the capital from the Highlands, and from isolated villages, in search of work and so would have no family in Edinburgh to enquire after their whereabouts. One morning, Burke even had the gall to approach a pair of policemen, who were taking an inebriated woman to the police station so that she could sleep off her over-indulgence. He lied that he knew her and offered to take her home. That evening he had another £10 to spend on drink.

By this time several of Dr Knox's students were beginning to talk openly about how their eminent professor was able to offer his class a regular supply of fresh specimens when his colleagues

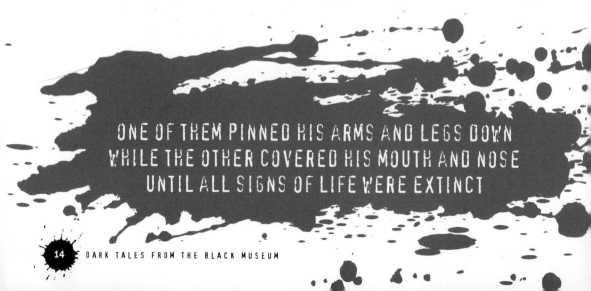

ONE OF THEM PINNED HIS ARMS AND LEGS DOWN WHILE THE OTHER COVERED HIS MOUTH AND NOSE UNTIL ALL SIGNS OF LIFE WERE EXTINCT

Among Edinburgh's floating population, there was no shortage of candidates for Burke and Hare's final ministrations

had to make do with a badly decomposed cadaver or, more often, none at all. Their disquiet grew when the body of a local prostitute was delivered to the school. Those who had seen her on the previous day reported that she had looked lively and had been none the worse for drink. But no one dared raise the matter directly with Dr Knox. However, soon afterwards several students voiced their concerns when the body of a well-known local character known as 'Daft Jamie', a mentally retarded youth with a club foot, was placed on the dissecting slab. It was a matter of seconds before they started questioning how this young man had died so suddenly and conveniently within the reach of Burke and Hare, who by now were known to be the sole suppliers of specimens to Dr Knox. The professor confirmed their suspicions by first taking a scalpel to the club foot and then to Jamie's face, in order to eradicate his identifiable features. It was as good as a confession.

And still the students kept silent, fearing scandal and, quite possibly, the closure of the

In the early 19th century the Scottish capital was flowering, but it had its own dark underbelly of crime and deprivation

school. Knox, or someone else in authority, may even have raised the possibility that they might all be named as accomplices if the matter became public.

THE LAST VICTIM

On the morning of 29 October 1828, Burke sat drinking his morning draught in the local tavern when he overheard an old woman, Mary Docherty, talking to the barman in a thick Irish accent. He engaged her in conversation and then claimed that he came from the same part of the old country as herself. They might even be related, he told her. With these words he lured Mary back to his house in Tanner's Close, where she met his wife Helen and a couple who were lodging with them, James and

Ann Gray. A party was held in order to celebrate the happy chance meeting and the drinking and dancing continued long after the Grays left. They had gone to stay the night with William Hare and his common law wife Margaret, giving up their room to Mary Docherty just as Burke had hoped. At around midnight another occupant of the house was passing the Burkes' door when he thought he heard two men arguing and a woman's stifled cries of 'Murder!' and 'Get the police!', but when he hurried into the street he could not see a policeman. On returning to the house all was quiet, so he assumed it was a domestic quarrel and he went to bed.

The next morning the Grays returned to Burke's rooms and were surprised to learn that Mary had gone. They were told that she had been turned out of the house in the early hours by Helen, who had claimed that the old woman and her husband were becoming too friendly for comfort. If the Grays found the explanation absurd they did not say so, but their suspicions were aroused when Burke warned Ann not to go near the bed. He later yelled at her when she started towards it to fetch some potatoes stored underneath. As soon as they were alone in the room the Grays looked under the bed and were horrified to see the body of the old woman. As they raced from the house they ran into Helen, who asked them where they were going in such a hurry. James accused her of murder and told her that they were going to fetch the police, which sent her into a panic. She begged them not to do so. Then she offered to share the profits with them if they kept silent, which only infuriated them further. However, by the time the police were summoned the body had vanished. Without it, there were no grounds for arresting William and Helen Burke.

But then a neighbour informed the police that two men had been seen carrying a large tea chest from the house only an hour or so before. When questioned, William claimed that Mrs Docherty had left at 7 o'clock that morning, whereas Helen asserted that the old woman had departed at 7 o'clock that evening. The discrepancy in their stories was sufficient to have them brought in for further questioning. Word soon went around the West Port that murder most foul had been perpetrated at Tanner's Close and someone suggested that the authorities should pay a visit

BURKE WARNED ANN NOT TO GO NEAR THE BED. HE LATER YELLED AT HER WHEN SHE STARTED TOWARDS IT TO FETCH SOME POTATOES STORED UNDERNEATH

to the dissecting rooms of Dr Knox. There they found a body which was identified by James Gray as being that of Mary Docherty.

By nightfall William Hare and Margaret were also in custody. Their conflicting and inconsistent statements convinced the authorities that they were guilty, but there was no physical evidence and there were no eyewitnesses. All of the evidence was circumstantial. The Lord Advocate believed that most of the guilt lay with Burke, so in order to force the issue and secure a conviction, he offered Hare immunity if he testified against Burke and Helen. Hare seized the chance to save his own skin and he confessed to the crimes, which now included the killing of Daft Jamie and the prostitute Mary Paterson, bringing the total number of victims to 15.

BURKE'S TRIAL AND EXECUTION

The trial of William Burke began on Christmas Eve 1828, with Helen named as his accomplice in the killing of Mary Docherty. The prosecution case relied almost entirely on the eyewitness testimony of William and Margaret Hare, the statements made by the Grays —which affirmed that the body of an old woman had been hidden in the house but was then spirited away – and the testimony of the lodger who had heard a woman crying 'Murder!' earlier that evening. Helen Burke's solicitor argued that she had been the woman who had cried out in horror when she had witnessed the old woman's death. He went on to say that the fact that she had been seen in the company of several of the victims did not prove that she was implicated in their deaths. It was a poor defence, but it sowed the seed of reasonable doubt.

On Christmas morning the jury returned with its verdicts. Burke was guilty, but the case against Helen was 'not proven', a uniquely Scottish verdict which implied that the accused had escaped imprisonment only because there was insufficient evidence to secure a conviction. On hearing the sentence Burke embraced Helen and wept.

'You are out of the scrape,' he said.

In the following weeks Burke made two formal confessions, which were published in broadsheets and sold by hawkers on the street corners of the city. Damned by his own words and abandoned by his accomplice, William Burke resigned himself to his fate. On 28 January 1829 he was led through

HARE SEIZED THE CHANCE TO SAVE HIS OWN SKIN AND CONFESSED TO THE CRIMES, WHICH NOW INCLUDED THE KILLING OF DAFT JAMIE AND MARY PATERSON

the jeering crowds who surged around the scaffold on the Lawnmarket. They called for Hare and Dr Knox to share his fate.

THE AFTERMATH

Remarkably, the eminent anatomist escaped prosecution, but was hounded by stone-throwing crowds at his home and at the medical college. The popularity of his classes dwindled significantly in the weeks and months after the trial. He applied for vacant posts at Edinburgh University Medical School, but he was rejected twice.

Eventually he left for London, where he obtained a position at a cancer hospital. He died in 1862. Although Burke swore that Knox had known nothing of the method by which the corpses were obtained, it seems implausible that a renowned anatomist would not have recognized the signs of a violent – or at least unnatural – death when dissecting the bodies.

The body of William Burke was taken down from the scaffold and delivered to the medical college, where it was dismembered in full view of the students who had attended the dissection of his victims. His skeleton was then put on public display in the college museum, together with his death mask and several items made from his tanned skin. It proved an effective deterrent. The incidence of grave robbing rapidly declined and the practice was all but eradicated by the Anatomy Act of 1832, which permitted the regular supply of dead bodies for dissection.

Hare did not escape justice, however. Angry mobs pursued him and the two women, driving them out of Scotland and harassing them whenever they attempted to settle down. Margaret

Public hanging: Edinburgh's citizens crammed the High Street to witness the final minutes of William Burke

is thought to have eventually returned to Ireland, it was rumoured that Helen had gone to Australia and William Hare was last heard of in Carlisle. It is not known if there is any truth in the story that he was thrown into a lime pit by an angry mob, forcing him to end his days as a blind beggar on the streets of London.

THE BOY WHO NEVER CAME HOME –

GORDON AND SARAH NORTHCOTT

In the late 1920s the citizens of Los Angeles went to the movies several times a week. For the price of a ticket they bought into a fairy-tale world where good always triumphed over evil and every story had a happy ending. So when a local man and his mother were accused of kidnapping and butchering innocent children in their own back yard, the public refused to believe that they could be guilty of such horrific crimes. Even the police preferred to believe that the victims had merely run away from home. They went so far as to commit an innocent mother to a lunatic asylum rather than admit that a boy claiming to be her missing son could be lying in order to escape from his abusive parents.

DIGGING UP THE TRUTH

The whole sickening story began in September 1928 when a Canadian woman, Winnefred Clark, contacted the United States federal authorities to report that her 15-year-old son Sanford had been abducted by his own uncle. The boy had apparently gone to stay with Gordon Stewart Northcott two years earlier with his mother's blessing, but a series of strange letters, supposedly written by the boy, was sufficiently unsettling for Winnefred to send her daughter Jessie to California to investigate. Jessie returned to confirm their worst fears. Gordon was sexually abusing the boy. He had even made an attempted assault on her, but she had fought him off and escaped.

The federal authorities wasted no time in raiding Northcott's poultry farm, only to find that 'Uncle Gordon' and his mother, Sarah Louise, had vanished, leaving the boy to fend for himself. When interviewed, Sanford claimed that he had been forced to witness the rape and murder of other boys and had even participated in their abduction, in order to save his own skin. He could see that

> GORDON WAS SEXUALLY ABUSING THE BOY. HE HAD EVEN MADE AN ATTEMPTED SEXUAL ASSAULT ON JESSIE, BUT SHE ESCAPED

Gordon Northcott and his mother Sarah Louise, who perhaps in an effort to gain sympathy also claimed to be his grandmother

the detectives doubted his incredible story so he promised to show them where the bodies were buried. Sure enough, he led them to two hastily dug graves, where human remains were unearthed. Two axes with matted blood and human hair on their blades were also recovered from the site and other body fragments were found scattered elsewhere on the farm. But hampered by primitive forensic techniques, investigators were unable to identify the victims. All they could say for certain was that the remains were those of male children and that they had met a violent end.

Other incriminating items were found elsewhere on the property. There were letters from another abductee and Boy Scout badges belonging to brothers Lewis and Nelson Winslow, who had been kidnapped on their way home in May. However, there was no sign of 9-year-old Walter Collins who had disappeared on his way to a cinema in Lincoln Heights, Los Angeles, on 10 March. Witnesses had reported seeing a boy's dead body wrapped in newspaper on the back seat of a car driven by a 'foreign-looking' couple on that day, but the car's occupants had given their pursuers the slip.

'TRY HIM OUT'

The Los Angeles police force was looking pretty incompetent by now and it needed to show results, but Captain J.J. Jones overstepped the mark by a mile when he attempted to convince distraught Christine Collins that another boy was her son and that she was simply too upset to recognize

No single complete body was ever found on the farm, but there may have been as many as 20 victims. No one knows

him! Arthur Hutchins had his own reasons for masquerading as the missing child – he had run away from his own hated stepmother – but Jones did not question his story. He continued to insist that Arthur Hutchins was Walter Collins and he accused Christine Collins of denying it in order to embarrass his department. She should take the boy home and 'try him out' for a few weeks, he said, until she came to her senses. Even though the poor woman returned three weeks later with documentary proof that the boy in her care was not Walter – she had brought her son's dental records and sworn statements from several people who

had known him – it was not enough. Jones had her committed to a mental institution under a provision that gave senior police officers the power to institutionalize 'troublesome witnesses'.

Handwriting analysis finally exposed Arthur Hutchins' charade and he was reunited with his stepmother. Captain Jones was forced to free Christine Collins, but an apology was not forthcoming.

THE QUESTIONS REMAIN

Meanwhile the killers of Walter Collins had split up in the hope of eluding the police, but they were captured at separate locations in Canada and brought to trial. Under interrogation, Gordon Northcott hinted at having killed nine boys, possibly even 20, but in the event he only confessed to five murders, including the Winslow brothers and Walter Collins. Northcott's mother, Sarah Louise, freely admitted her part in the killings but later stalled for time by denying that she had known the victims.

However, her grandson, young Sanford, whose abduction had uncovered the whole sordid story, told detectives that his grandmother had told him that they would each strike the child with the axe so that they would equally share the guilt. This seems to have been an attempt to frighten Sanford into staying quiet. He was later convicted of having played a minor role in the murders and was sent to a youth offenders' institution for several years.

Gordon attempted to defend himself at his trial in January 1929, but his clumsy efforts to convince the jury of his intellectual superiority only served to alienate them. They became convinced that he was both a sexual sadist and a pathological liar. His mother was no help.

On the stand she claimed to be his grandmother. She told the court a bizarre story of how her husband had raped their daughter Winnefred, who had later given birth to Gordon. If this was intended to elicit the jury's sympathies and explain Gordon's pathology it did not work. By this time the all-male jury could take no more of the defendants' fantasies and they were nauseous from hearing the sickening details of their crimes. They found both defendants guilty. Sarah Louise Northcott was sentenced to life imprisonment and her son Gordon was sentenced to death. He was hanged on 2 October 1930.

In an effort to erase all memory of the crimes the citizens of Wineville petitioned to change the name of their town to Mira Loma. But one person who could not forgive or forget was Christine Collins. She instigated proceedings against the Los Angeles Police Department for false imprisonment. But although she won her case Captain Jones refused to pay her restitution and Jones and his superior, Chief Davis, were reinstated.

Christine managed to get permission to meet face to face with Gordon Northcott before his execution, but he cruelly denied that he had abducted her son and she, incredibly, believed him. She spent the rest of her days searching in vain for the boy who never came home.

YOUNG SANFORD TOLD DETECTIVES HIS GRANDMOTHER HAD TOLD HIM THAT THEY WOULD EACH STRIKE THE CHILD WITH THE AXE SO THAT THEY WOULD EQUALLY SHARE THE GUILT

TILL DEATH DO US PART –

BONNIE AND CLYDE

The 'Roaring Twenties' and the early 1930s are remembered as an era of glitzy jazz clubs, flappers, fast cars and gangsters with money to burn and no respect for the law. Big shots like Al Capone had grown fat on the back of the Volstead Act, a universally unpopular law that prohibited the manufacture and sale of alcohol. It had been passed by Congress to appease a vociferous lobby of moral crusaders – religious do-gooders who wanted to save the souls of America's youth, which they feared were being corrupted by the demon drink.

But the new law instead gave rise to an insatiable thirst for illegal liquor and created a new breed of criminal – men who grew so rich by selling bootleg hooch that they could afford to pay corrupt law enforcement officials and politicians to look the other way.

Prohibition was still in force when the Wall Street Crash of 1929 dragged the United States into the Great Depression, thereby ending the 'American Dream' of prosperity and opportunity for all. Overnight, thousands of businesses went bust and millions of workers lost their jobs. Day by day, the queues grew longer at the soup kitchens and 'bread lines', and at the height of the Depression the unemployed camped in Washington's parks to bring their plight to the attention of Capitol Hill. Only the gangsters and the banks remained immune, or so it seemed.

In the rural backwaters of America, many families found themselves impoverished and

PROHIBITION DID NOT SAVE AMERICA. INSTEAD, IT GAVE RISE TO AN INSATIABLE THIRST FOR ILLEGAL LIQUOR AND A NEW BREED OF CRIMINAL

One for the family album: Bonnie and Clyde helped inflate their own myth with pictures such as this

homeless as the banks foreclosed on farms and businesses with ruthless indifference. Tested to the limits of their endurance, the God-fearing folks of the Great Plains turned to their Christian faith for answers, but it seemed that the good Lord, too, had turned away from them.

In 1930 a terrible drought struck the region with the enormity of a biblical plague, turning the once fertile farmlands into what became known as the Dust Bowl. Huge dust storms stripped the land of its top soil, leaving the plains as uninhabitable as a desert.

PUBLIC ENEMIES

In this climate of despair and and disillusionment more than a few country boys turned to crime – and got away with it, too, so long as they kept within the county boundaries. But as soon as they crossed the state lines their crimes became a federal felony, which gave the FBI the authority to hunt them down. Bank robbers such as John Dillinger, 'Baby Face' Nelson and 'Pretty Boy' Floyd became unlikely folk heroes, stealing from the rich and redistributing their newly acquired wealth to the poor, while leading J. Edgar Hoover and his G-men a merry dance across the states.

Bonnie and Clyde were high-spirited young lovers with no roots, no responsibilities and a fatal belief in their own immortality, so robbing banks while sticking a middle digit up at the authorities must have seemed like a great adventure. Besides, it was the only work that paid a steady wage. They knew that it could all only end in imprisonment or death, but they must have felt that they had nothing to lose. Fate had dealt them loaded dice from the start.

And fate, it seemed, had also had a hand in their meeting. Just before Christmas 1929 Clyde was visiting the sister of a friend in Dallas, who had slipped on the ice and broken her arm. Bonnie was in the kitchen mixing hot chocolate when Clyde walked in to see what all the noise was about. The attraction was instant.

Bonnie Elizabeth Parker (born 1 October 1910 in Rowena, Texas) was petite – she was just under 5 feet tall – and she had strawberry blonde hair and freckles. But although the local hicks might have found her attractive, she did not possess the qualities that would hook the kind of man who could keep her in the manner to which she wished to become accustomed. She had the brains to get decent grades in high school, but she was painfully aware that she would never amount to anything unless she could force people to sit up and take notice of her. After Bonnie's father died, her mother moved the family to Cement City, where they lived with Bonnie's grandparents. Bonnie soon eloped with local tough guy Roy Thornton, a young man who was as impatient to get rich as she was. But he was stupid enough to get caught and was sentenced to a long stretch in prison. Dejected, and determined never to rely on a man again, Bonnie returned home and took a job as a waitress to make ends meet.

BROWN-EYED HANDSOME MAN

At around the same time, Clyde Chestnut Barrow was getting an apprenticeship in burglary in the company of his brother Marvin Ivan, known to all as 'Buck'. One night the pair broke into a store and stole the safe, loading it on to the back of a truck they had taken earlier that night. Buck's luck ran out when he crashed a stolen car into a lamppost while trying to evade the police. He stubbornly refused to name his partner, who had escaped through a maze of back alleys in the dark, and so was given a stiff sentence, which left Clyde as the family's main breadwinner. Predictably, Clyde returned to burglary and shoplifting, making no effort to hide his face from those who lived to identify him.

Clyde had one asset, though – his looks. He was only 5 feet 7 inches tall, but he was brown-eyed and slim. His large ears, his predominant feature, were made all the more noticeable by his short brown hair. Although he was shy and awkward in the company of strangers, Clyde felt at ease around Bonnie, who saw in him a chance to kick off the dust of the small town and live the sort of life she had only seen in the movies.

Bonnie liked to believe that her backwoods beau had a passion for her and her alone, but Clyde's smouldering emotions were limited to self-loathing and a blind hatred for anyone who got in his way. He hated being a hick, a dirt poor farmer's boy from a small town in Texas, who had to share a room with seven brothers and sisters above a petrol station in West Dallas. His father had found work there after being turned off their farm. Years of poverty had embittered Clyde and left him with no feelings for anyone but himself. It also seems likely that he was confused by his own sexuality. He was in constant turmoil because of his apparent inability to have a normal physical relationship with Bonnie. Bonnie was content just to be with him, but she must have wondered why he did not paw her and pester her to have sex, like the other local boys.

At their first meeting they talked late into the night. Clyde confided that he and his friends were on the run, wanted for hold-ups in the neighbouring counties of Waco and McClennan. If she didn't believe him she could come with them on their next job and see him in action, a dare she readily accepted. Now he had an admirer to dangle on his arm, and a pretty one at that, which would make the other gang members jealous. It is said that Bonnie offered to drive the getaway car, but before the Barrow gang got a chance to make a name for itself Clyde was arrested and held for trial at the Waco County Courthouse. It was a formidable fortress that no ordinary petty hoodlum could

CLYDE'S SMOULDERING EMOTIONS WERE LIMITED TO SELF-LOATHING AND A BLIND HATRED FOR ANYONE WHO GOT IN HIS WAY. HE HATED BEING A HICK

have escaped from, but the authorities had not reckoned with the determination of 19-year-old Bonnie Parker. She stole a gun and smuggled it in to Clyde during visiting hours. The evening after the trial Clyde and his cell mate Frank Turner broke out by disarming the guard at gunpoint and locking him in the cell.

ON THE RUN

The pair evaded local police patrols and headed off for Illinois, where they enjoyed a brief spell robbing fruit stands, petrol stations and train depots. But they were soon back in custody after a witness noted the numberplate of their stolen car and reported it to the police. That was a valuable lesson Clyde determined never to forget. When he began his criminal career in earnest with Bonnie they were sure to change numberplates immediately after each job.

Back in Waco, Clyde was immediately hauled before a judge who meted out a stiff 14-year sentence with hard labour, to be served at the notorious Eastham Prison Farm, just north of Huntsville. Good-looking young 'punks' (the inmates' term for a male sexual partner) endured

continual harassment by older prisoners, as well as routine beatings by sadistic guards. In his desperation to get out of Eastham at any cost, Clyde persuaded another prisoner to fake an accident which cost him two toes. On 8 February 1932 he was discharged due to injury, which allowed him to hobble on crutches to freedom and into the waiting arms of Bonnie.

Prison had not cowed Clyde Barrow. If anything, the experience had fuelled his intense hatred of the law – so much so that he now sought revenge, regardless of the risk to himself. Teaming up with former inmates Ralph Fults and Ray Hamilton he planned a series of stick-ups in small towns across the state, beginning with a hardware store in Kaufman, which just happened to be right across the street from the courthouse. Clyde's arrogance was shortlived, however, because a night watchmen set off the alarm. The gang made their getaway by the skin of their teeth, dumping Bonnie by the roadside to save her from capture. But she did not appreciate the gesture – she wanted to ride alongside Clyde and if necessary shoot it out and share the loot. She got her chance shortly after the Kaufman heist when Fults and Hamilton were

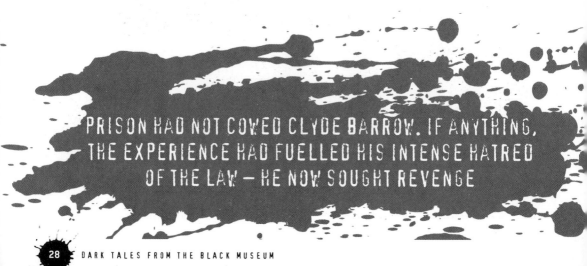

PRISON HAD NOT COWED CLYDE BARROW. IF ANYTHING, THE EXPERIENCE HAD FUELLED HIS INTENSE HATRED OF THE LAW – HE NOW SOUGHT REVENGE

Gangster's Moll: Bonnie adopts a pose that was to be aped in Hollywood movies such as *Gun Crazy*

Anguished mother Mrs Emma Parker and Bonnie's sister, Billy Mace, photographed in Dallas in 1935

arrested in separate incidents, the latter after accidentally shooting dead a store owner. This nailed Clyde as an accomplice to murder and made it only a matter of time before the law caught up with him.

A TIGHT SPOT

'I'm just going on 'til they get me. Then I'm out like Lottie's eye.'

CLYDE BARROW, IN A LETTER TO HIS SISTER

In the summer of 1932, just before Hamilton's arrest, a luckless hoodlum almost cost Bonnie and Clyde their liberty. Clyde, Bonnie, Hamilton and one of Hamilton's buddies, Everett Milligan, were driving through Oklahoma when they spotted an open air dance, so they decided to stretch their legs and have a little fun. But no sooner had they stepped unsteadily on to the dance floor, clearly under the influence of illegal hooch, than a couple of local cops approached them and demanded to know why they were drunk in public.

Clyde and Hamilton instinctively went for their weapons, firing at almost point-blank range. They wounded one officer in the gut and killed the other on the spot with a bullet in the throat. In the confusion, Milligan fled. He was captured by a group of irate locals who held him until the police arrived to arrest him. When Milligan identified the shooters as 'The Barrow Gang', an all-state alert was immediately issued. The orders were to bring them in dead or alive.

But Bonnie and Clyde were already heading for the state line, with Hamilton in the back seat. Bonnie suggested that they should hole up at her aunt Nettie's place in Carlsbad, New Mexico, which was so far from the site of the shooting that no lawman would think of looking for them there. Unfortunately for the lovers, Clyde was in a hurry. He raced through the town at top speed, arousing the suspicions of local patrolman Joe Johns, who noted the out of state plates.

Johns radioed in with the licence number and when he was told it was a stolen car he followed it to the home of Nettie Stamps. Nettie watched from an upstairs window as the officer approached the front door and she looked on helplessly as Clyde disarmed the officer and walked him to their waiting car.

Patrolman Johns was missing, presumed murdered, for several days and then to everyone's relief he turned up very much alive and unharmed. He was able to tell the newspapers a wild story about how he was kidnapped and forced to pose for photographs with Bonnie and Clyde.

GUN CRAZY

Clyde's hair-trigger temper was now almost a natural reflex. He would react like a cornered animal, shooting anyone who looked at him sideways or made a smart remark. In Sherman, Texas, a store owner, Howard Hill, made a sarcastic comment while handing over the day's takings and was shot dead. Clyde was clearly a sociopath, but he was shrewd and cautious when it came to saving his own skin. He deliberately targeted border towns so that Bonnie and he could escape across state lines when the law got too close for comfort. The pair also steered clear of motels, preferring to sleep out in the open during summer and in vacated log cabins whenever they could find one.

But the legend of Bonnie and Clyde belies the fact that they were failures at their chosen profession. By the winter of 1932 it had finally dawned on the couple that robbing tills would never net them the wealth they wanted. The obvious next step was to hold up a bank. Bonnie offered to case the first place they chose, the Oswego Bank in Carthage, Missouri, and she did a fine job of memorizing the layout. But when the

CLYDE'S HAIR-TRIGGER TEMPER WAS NOW ALMOST A NATURAL REFLEX. HE WOULD REACT LIKE A CORNERED ANIMAL, SHOOTING ANYONE WHO LOOKED AT HIM day came Clyde pulled out his .38 in full view of a guard, who let fly before he could return fire. With bullets whizzing past his head, Clyde scurried out with nothing more than the handful of dollar bills he had been able to snatch from the teller.

The second job was even more embarrassing. Dismissing the preliminary look around as a waste of time, Clyde rushed in with guns drawn only to find himself in a branch that had closed down some years before. There was not a soul in the place, the tills were covered in cobwebs and the clock had long ceased to tick.

A NEW RECRUIT

Homesick at Christmas, the couple returned to Dallas where they snatched fleeting meetings with their families in secret locations. When they left they took with them 16-year-old W.D. Jones, who had pestered Clyde to let him join the gang. Clyde had finally relented, if only to shut the boy up. Though only a teenager, Jones was powerfully built. He could drive a car and handle himself in a fight, which made him quite an asset – or so they hoped. In practice, W.D. proved to be a lethal liability. On Christmas Day the three drove into the town of Temple, cruising the streets in search of a new car to steal. W.D. spotted a brand new Ford V8 Coupe. He boasted that it would enable him to outrace any pursuing patrol car, but when he climbed into the driver's seat he could not start it. Exasperated, Clyde ordered Bonnie to take the wheel of their own car while he pushed Jones aside and attempted to get the now flooded engine to start. The noise of the stuttering Ford brought the local inhabitants to their front windows and the owner racing out into the street. He grabbed Clyde by the tie and clung on

as the Ford Coupe kicked into life. Clyde put his foot to the floor. A moment later, as the car accelerated, there was the sickening sound of a gunshot from within; the owner loosened his hold and slid to the ground.

Things went from bad to worse back in Dallas; in the spring of 1933, when a police officer was fatally wounded as the gang shot their way out of an ambush arranged by the authorities. Following this change in police tactics, the gang broke into a government armoury and tooled up to the nines with submachine guns, automatic rifles and gas grenades. Shortly afterwards, they kidnapped a motorcycle cop who had been pursuing them through Springfield, Illinois, and then forced him to steal a car battery and fit it for them.

But the law would not allow itself to be made a fool of and that year the noose tightened around Bonnie and Clyde.

BREAK-OUT

In March 1933 Clyde was reunited with his brother Buck, who had finally been released from Huntsville and was now married to a highly strung young woman named Blanche. The brothers thought it would be fun to rent an apartment together and party while the law chased their own shadows. They chose a secluded furnished apartment above a double garage in family-friendly Freeman Park in Joplin. Freeman Park had promised privacy and anonymity, but the gang had not reckoned with their neighbours' insatiable curiosity. Local residents wasted no time in reporting seeing the men carrying armfuls of weapons into the building and they also observed that the curtains were drawn day and night.

Ivy 'Buck' Barrow posing in front of the gang's getaway vehicle that was now a mobile arsenal with ever-changing licence plates

Being cooped up in the flat had made the brothers grow restless and they soon tired of playing cards, listening to the radio and reading the newspapers. Why not rob the local bank? No one knew them around there and they had the perfect hideout to come back to. What they did not know was that the police had the premises under surveillance following the tip-offs, so when Clyde, Buck and Bonnie returned from their 'outing' in a stolen car the authorities were able to match them to the descriptions of the suspects fleeing the scene.

On the morning of 13 April, the police blocked the garage doors with one of their vehicles and began to surround the building. Then Clyde's face suddenly appeared at the window. Someone had made too much noise and gang members were now alerted. Before the cops could run for cover, a full-scale gun battle was under way. Two officers were felled with the first shots, but incredibly none of the gang was hurt. They returned fire through the shattered windows while bullets whizzed and ricocheted all around them, sending a lethal spray of shrapnel and glass in every direction. Blanche became hysterical and ran around screaming, accompanied by the yelping of a puppy tucked into her apron pocket. There was nothing for it but to attempt a break-out.

Staying around to fight would be suicide, so Clyde ordered them all down into the garage, where they piled into their Ford. All except Blanche, that is, who ran out of the back door and across the lawn before Buck could grab her.

Bonnie kept her head down, hugging Clyde around the waist as he started the car. He drove it clean through the closed garage doors, brushing aside the police car that had blocked the entrance. The cops scattered in every direction, recovering in time to see the getaway car careering down the road. Clyde pulled up at the kerb just long enough for Buck to haul his new bride inside and then off he sped, leaving the dazed lawmen wondering what had hit them. But now at least they knew the identity of the two new members of the gang. Among the debris in the apartment they found Blanche's purse and Buck's parole papers.

A MOMENT OF LIGHT RELIEF

In Ruston, Louisiana, Clyde ordered W.D. to steal a black Chevrolet that had caught his eye and meet up with the gang later. But again the boy bungled the theft. He took so long to get the car into gear that the owner, H. Darby Dillard, was able to borrow his girlfriend's car and take off in hot pursuit with the girl, Sophie Stone, going along for the ride. At the rendezvous point Dillard leapt out of Sophie's car and confronted W.D., but he was surprised to see the boy grin and pull out a gun. Then Clyde, Buck, Bonnie and Blanche pulled up behind them and bundled Dillard and Sophie into their car at gunpoint.

'We're the Barrow gang,' Bonnie informed them proudly.

The 'hostages' grew pale and silent, but they soon relaxed when their kidnappers offered to buy them hamburgers. They also promised to drop them off safely once Clyde got tired of driving the new Chevvy. The atmosphere lightened and the conversation turned to the things they all had in common. But sometime later someone asked Dillard what he did for a living.

'I'm an undertaker,' he told them.

They ditched him and Sophie at the side of the road, giving them a few dollars to get a ride back to town. It was an unnerving portent of their impending fate.

ACCIDENT

As the gang raced down Highway 203 towards Wellington, Clyde failed to see a sign warning that a bridge had collapsed. When he saw the gaping chasm ahead it was too late. He braked hard, sending the car into a skid and throwing everyone out into the road. All escaped unscathed except Bonnie, who suffered a vicious-looking gash to her leg. Help was at hand, though, in the form of a farmer, who carried the injured girl back to his home where his wife tended the wound as best she could. W.D. was put on lookout as Buck and Clyde argued about what to do next, but the boy screwed up again when the farmer went to phone the police from a neighbour's house.

'I thought he was going to feed the animals,' W.D. whimpered when Clyde bawled him out.

The gang took off before the law arrived, with the injured Bonnie moaning in pain in the front seat beside Clyde. Blanche whined about how much trouble they were in and W.D. continually complained that he was hungry. Evading road blocks, the gang eventually pulled in to the Twin Cities Tourist Camp in Arkansas, from where Clyde called a doctor. It was a risky business, but Bonnie was clearly in considerable pain and might lose the leg if something was not done to clean the wound and reduce the risk of infection. The doctor believed the story that she had been injured by an exploding oil stove and after doing what he could he recommended that she be taken to hospital. That was obviously out of the question, but Clyde agreed to hire a nurse to attend to her, whose fees were to be paid out of the proceeds of the next two robberies. W.D. and Buck were dispatched to rob a bank in Alma and then a store in nearby Fayetteville, while Clyde sat at the bedside of his beloved, who continually called for her mother while sinking in and out of consciousness. When W.D. and Buck returned they had the money but they were also the bearers of more bad news. They had killed a United States marshal in the grocery store hold-up and now the heat really was on.

But they had a lucky break when they chose their next getaway car. It was owned by a doctor who, quite by chance, had left his medical bag in the vehicle on the day it was driven away by the Barrow gang.

PLATTE CITY SHOOT-OUT

The gang's run of luck ended on 18 July 1933. Bonnie was still unable to walk unaided when they rolled into the Red Crown Tourist Camp just outside Platte City, Missouri, but most of the gang would soon be in far worse shape. In a virtual re-run of the Freeman Park shoot-out, the gang found themselves surrounded by dozens of heavily armed officers, while the garage door was barred by an armoured truck. With Clyde at the wheel of their car the gang burst through the garage door, smashing it to matchwood. Clyde then rammed the truck, giving himself just enough room to squeeze past the vehicle and scatter the cordon of armed men. As they roared away, W.D. raked the driver's door of the armoured car with

THE GANG FOUND THEMSELVES SURROUNDED BY DOZENS OF HEAVILY ARMED OFFICERS, WHILE THE GARAGE DOOR WAS BARRED BY AN ARMOURED TRUCK shotgun pellets, putting the officer out of action so that he could not pursue them. But in the mayhem that would have put a Peckinpah movie to shame, Buck was mortally wounded in the head, Blanche was blinded in one eye and W.D. was hit in the shoulder.

When the gang made a dawn stop in Dexfield Park, so that they could lick their wounds, they were again surrounded, this time by about a hundred men armed with hunting rifles, all eager for a share of the reward money. Clyde was winged and Bonnie received a stinging flesh wound, but the pair of them managed to stagger through the woods and vanish among the outlying corn fields, leaving Buck and Blanche behind. Buck bled to death three days later, with half of his head blown away. Blanche survived and was subsequently sentenced to 10 years in prison. W.D. disappeared, but he was later arrested in Houston.

By autumn 1933 even the gang's families had resigned themselves to the inevitable. Both the Barrow and the Parker clans had visited a local funeral parlour to make the necessary arrangements, though Clyde and Bonnie were still on the run.

END OF THE ROAD

They did not stop running and robbing until 6 May 1934, when they met up with their folks in a rural backwater outside Dallas to enjoy a final family picnic. Bonnie knew the net was closing in and that it was only a matter of time before they met their end. She tried to console her mother.

'Now, Mama, don't get upset... It's coming. You know it. I know it... Mama, when they kill us, don't ever say anything ugly about Clyde.'

That's when Bonnie handed her mother a poem she had recently written, celebrating their notoriety. When the couple said their goodbyes everyone knew they would not see them again – alive, that is.

Henry Methvin, a car thief, had been sprung out of Eastham Prison Farm by Bonnie and Clyde a few months earlier, along with their old gang member Ray Hamilton. But Methvin was to hasten their end by betraying them. During the break-out a guard had been killed, prompting the authorities to hire bounty hunter Frank Hamer to mete out the wages of sin to the perpetrators. The former Texas ranger already had 80 notches on his gun, as well as a reputation for bringing back the bodies of those he

FRANK HAMER ALREADY HAD 80 NOTCHES ON HIS GUN, AS WELL AS A REPUTATION FOR BRINGING BACK THE BODIES OF THOSE HE HAD BEEN HIRED TO TRACK DOWN

Overkill: Bonnie and Clyde's V-8 Ford sedan was punctured by 167 bullets; there was no chance of anyone emerging alive

had been hired to track down. When Methvin heard that Hamer was on their trail he became a bundle of nerves. Shortly afterwards, the Barrow gang hid out at the farm owned by Iverson (Iver) Methvin, Henry's father, in Acadia, Louisiana. While they were there Henry begged his father to make a deal with the law so he wouldn't end up on a mortuary slab beside Bonnie and Clyde. Iver Methvin saw a chance to secure a lighter sentence for his boy and also get some reward money, so he wasted no time in contacting the authorities. He cut a deal for his son in exchange for setting up an ambush.

Early on the morning of 23 May 1934 Iver Methvin parked his truck by a ditch on the Sailes Road, knowing that the fugitives would have to pass that way on their way back from their regular forays into town. He was confident that they would recognize his vehicle and pull over to see what the trouble was. As Methvin senior paced nervously beside his vehicle Frank Hamer and his men waited under the moss-covered trees that lined the narrow road. There would be no warning this time. Experience had shown them that Bonnie and Clyde would shoot it out rather than surrender.

Men in hats: taking their lead from Bonnie and Clyde, the lawmen liked to document their triumphs too,
Standing (l to r): Ted Hinton, Prentiss Oakley, B.M. 'Maney' Gault; sitting: Bob Alcorn, Henderson Jordan and Frank Hamer

At 9.15 am a beige 1934 Ford came hurtling down the dirt road, screeching to a halt as it came upon the abandoned truck. From his hidden vantage point Dallas police officer Ted Hinton recognized the silhouette of Clyde Barrow, who was craning his neck in search of the driver.

'It's him!' Hinton mouthed to Hamer, who immediately yelled, 'Shoot!'

Hinton described the last moments of the outlaws in his co-authored account of the killing, *Ambush*.

'... *Bonnie screams, and I fire and everyone fires... a drumbeat of shells knifes through the steel body of the car, and glass is shattering. For a fleeting instant, the car seems to melt and hang in a kind of eerie and animated suspension...*

Clyde is slumped forward, the back of his head a mat of blood... I scramble over the hood of the car and throw open the door on Bonnie's side. The impression will linger with me from this instant – I see her falling out of the opened door, a beautiful and petite young girl... and I smell a light perfume against the burned-cordite smell of gunpowder...'

Hinton recognized Bonnie at once. She had served him when she had worked as a waitress at Marco's Diner in Dallas back in 1929.

The story of Bonnie and Clyde had come full circle – to a dead end.

And Bonnie's prediction had come to pass.

Bonnie and Clyde revelled in their image as modern-day bandit lovers and they took every opportunity to be photographed on the run from the authorities, embracing or kissing as they proudly showed off their arsenal of weapons or their latest getaway car.

Over two years they had terrorized five states – Texas, Oklahoma, Missouri, Louisiana, and New Mexico – killing anyone who got in their way. They gloried in their weaponry and did not give a second thought to the carnage they left in their wake.

'SOMEDAY THEY'LL GO DOWN TOGETHER
AND THEY'LL BURY THEM SIDE BY SIDE
TO A FEW IT'LL BE GRIEF, TO THE LAW A RELIEF
BUT IT'S DEATH FOR BONNIE AND CLYDE.'

'THE STORY OF BONNIE AND CLYDE', BONNIE PARKER, MAY 1934

THE HONEYMOON KILLERS –

MARTHA BECK AND RAYMOND FERNANDEZ

Their story could have been ripped from between the covers of the lurid pulp magazines of the period, but every detail revealed in a humid, crowded court room in the Bronx during the summer of 1949 was absolutely true. Raymond Martinez Fernandez and his corpulent lover Martha Beck had lured 17 sex-starved single women to their lair and murdered them for their money. Ironically, for a couple who preyed on 'lonely hearts' they were notoriously cold, calculating and emotionless. After one particularly brutal slaying, when Martha murdered a victim's two-year-old daughter by drowning her in a bath, the pair of them went to the cinema, where they consumed a bucket of popcorn and a gallon of lemonade.

They were an odd couple for sure. Thirty-four-year-old Raymond was Hawaii-born, swarthy, slim and a smart dresser, but balding. He was an old-time Lothario who appealed to lonely middle-aged women, but he would have been laughed at if he had tried his obsequious charms on a pretty young girl. He nevertheless boasted that women found him irresistible and that his sexual prowess and charisma were the manifestation of his voodoo powers. His corpulent lover, 29-year-old Martha Beck (born Martha Seabrook), was certainly under

his spell. During the long hours of interrogation after their arrest on 28 February 1949, she sat in silent admiration of her lover and freely admitted that she was his sex slave.

MARTHA'S EARLY LIFE

Her psychosis was due, it was said, to a glandular abnormality that had accelerated her development, so that she became a sexually active woman while she was still a child. But the condition had also affected her physical development, making her obese. Her adolescence was abnormal, to say

> AFTER ONE SLAYING, THEY WENT TO THE CINEMA WHERE THEY CONSUMED A BUCKET OF POPCORN AND A GALLON OF LEMONADE

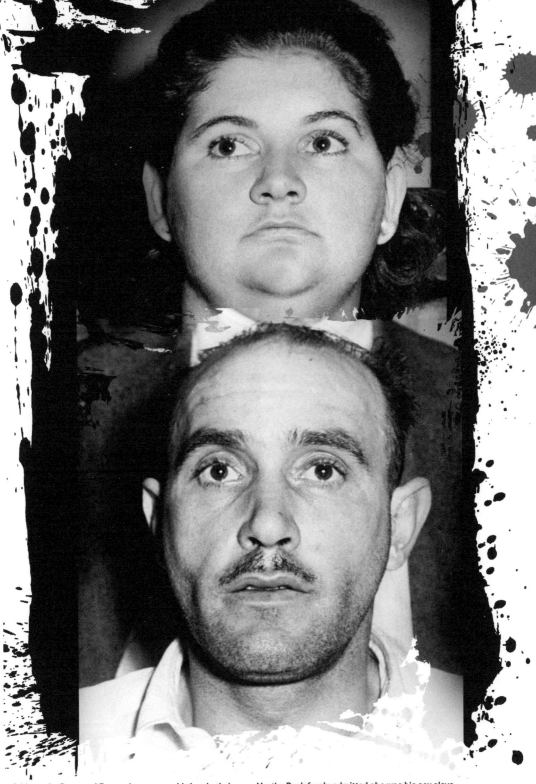

Odd couple: Raymond Fernandez was an old-time Latin lover – Martha Beck freely admitted she was his sex slave

Divorcee Jane Thompson was persuaded to accompany Fernandez on a cruise to Spain – she never came back alive

in 1942 where she spent her evenings cruising the bars in order to pick up servicemen for sex. When she discovered that she was pregnant she confronted the father, who threatened to kill himself rather than marry her. To save face, she concocted a story about how she had married a naval officer who had been sent overseas. She proudly showed off the ring to her neighbours, but she had in fact bought it herself. After the baby arrived and there was still no sign of the fictitious father, Martha sent herself a fake telegram notifying her of his 'death' on duty. She then received the sympathy she had craved for so long. Shortly afterwards she met a bus driver, Alfred Beck, who made her pregnant, married her out of sympathy and then left her six months later. Now with two young children to look after – Anthony and Carmen – she withdrew into a fantasy world nourished by trashy romantic magazines and dime novelettes. A new job as a nurse at a children's hospital might have been the saving of her, because she worked well and was promoted to superintendent, but her craving for love and sexual satisfaction would not be appeased through daydreams.

A CHANGED MAN

Raymond was a pleasant, amiable young man and a dutiful husband and father until a freak accident altered his personality. While serving aboard a freighter just after the war he was struck on the head by a steel hatch cover, which dented his skull causing irreparable brain damage. When he was eventually discharged from hospital in March 1946, his gentle affable personality had been replaced by a quick-tempered, irascible brooding nature and a compulsion to steal items of little value.

the least, because her mother continually chased away teenage boys with verbal abuse and threats of violence, then beat her daughter for encouraging them. Martha became reclusive, a condition which was exacerbated by her failure to find employment as a nurse, despite qualifying first in her class. She was forced to take a job in a funeral parlour where she worked nights, preparing female bodies for burial.

Desperately unhappy, she moved to California

The habit earned him a one-year prison sentence during which he shared a cell with a practitioner of voodoo, which gave him an obsession with the occult. On his release he went to live with his sister in Brooklyn, but he kept himself to himself. He complained of headaches and rarely left his room except to post letters to solitary women who had advertised in the lonely hearts columns of the national newspapers. When he met them, he seduced them and robbed them of their valuables, trusting that his victims would be too embarrassed to report the thefts to the police. They were humiliated but unharmed – that is, until Raymond claimed his first murder victim in November 1947.

She was divorcee Jane Thompson. He persuaded her to accompany him on a cruise to Spain, ostensibly to visit his wife and child, whom he had not seen since his accident. Mrs Thompson paid for their passage. When they arrived in Spain Raymond introduced Jane Thompson to his wife and at first the two women were on friendly terms. Then on the night of 7 November 1947 a violent disagreement took place between them after which Raymond was seen to leave Mrs Thompson's room in a hurry. The next morning Jane Thompson was found dead, apparently of natural causes. With no reason to suspect foul play, the Spanish authorities waived the need for an autopsy and she was buried with undue haste. Raymond then left his Spanish wife for the second time and returned to the United States, so that he could claim Mrs Thompson's New York apartment and belongings with the aid of a forged will. His criminal career had now begun in earnest.

LOVE LETTERS

On Christmas Day 1947 Martha received her one and only reply to an advertisement she had placed in the lonely hearts column of a national magazine. It was from a 'courteous and successful Spanish businessman' who had settled in New York and was now living in a bachelor apartment that was far too large for him alone. However, he hoped one day to share it with a wife. He piled on the sincerity with a trowel, adding that he had deduced from Martha's description that she had 'a full heart and a great capacity for comfort and love'. She responded by sending a group photograph of the hospital staff in which her squat 14-stone frame was discreetly hidden behind a row of colleagues. After a rapid exchange of letters Raymond requested a lock of hair. The love-struck Martha sent it willingly,

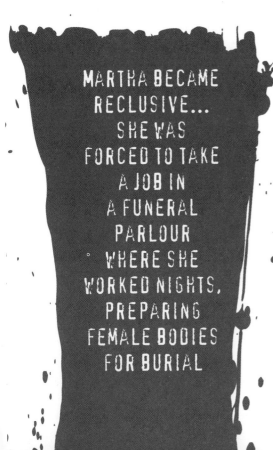

MARTHA BECAME RECLUSIVE... SHE WAS FORCED TO TAKE A JOB IN A FUNERAL PARLOUR WHERE SHE WORKED NIGHTS, PREPARING FEMALE BODIES FOR BURIAL

Janet Fay's body was buried at night in the basement of a rented house, paid for with money from the victim's bank account

assuming that it would be treasured as a love token. In fact, Raymond used it for a voodoo ritual, believing that it would bind Martha to him until he could rob her of whatever wealth he imagined she might possess.

But Martha was not to be fleeced and fooled so easily. When Raymond travelled down to Florida on 28 December it was lust at first sight, for her at least. If he was shocked by her appearance and the presence of two children whose existence she had not even hinted at, then he did not let on. He indulged her in fantasies of wedded bliss, but as soon as he was back in New York he wrote to tell her that any thoughts of marriage must have been a misunderstanding on her part. Martha was not to be shaken off so lightly. Packing a suitcase, she caught the next train to New York with her two kids in tow. When the unlikely looking Romeo answered the door on 18 January he found a new family camped on the front step. Evidently his voodoo charms must have been more potent than he had thought. He took them in against his better instincts and Martha went straight into her devoted slave routine. This convinced Raymond that he was on to a good thing if he could string her along without any further talk of marriage.

But the kids would have to go. Incredibly, Martha relented and one morning she dropped her two offspring off at the local Salvation Army shelter without so much as a note of explanation. It was as if they were two sacks of charity cast-offs. She did not see them again until she was in prison.

STRANGE DOUBLE ACT

Having proved Martha's unquestioning obedience, Raymond took her into his confidence. He explained the scam he was operating and together they found her a role to play in the scheme, one that would make his story more convincing. They scoured the country in the following months, systematically working through a list of would-be wives. Posing as either his sister or his sister-in-law, Martha played the role of chaperone. At one point she even slept in the marriage bed with the new bride, to prevent the couple from consummating their union. At this stage their crime was heinous but not homicidal. They fleeced the gullible and lived off the proceeds, but it rarely amounted to more than a few thousand dollars.

But at the beginning of 1949 Martha's jealousy took a vicious turn and she bludgeoned her lover's new bride to death with a hammer after strangling her with a scarf. Janet Fay was a devout Catholic whom Raymond had ensnared by appealing to her religious faith. He played the upright, moral Christian husband all the way to the altar, but when Martha walked in on them lying naked in bed on their wedding night Raymond demanded that Martha silence her in any way she could. It is not known if he struck Janet with the hammer and Martha strangled her or if it was the other way round. Maybe Martha committed the crime

alone, but that seems unlikely. In her confession she claimed to have no recollection of the killing. Whatever the truth, they both colluded in the cover-up. They wrapped the bloody corpse in towels and bed sheets and stored it in a closet and then they both went to sleep as if nothing had happened.

The next day they purchased a large trunk. After cramming the body into it they took it to the home

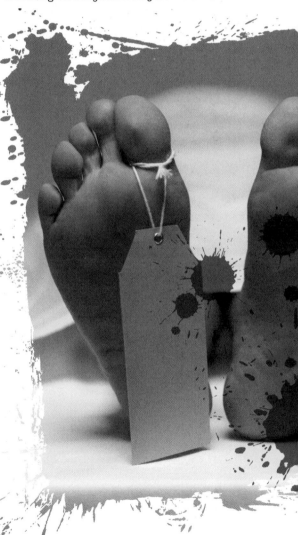

Early grave: no one knows exactly how many women ended up on the mortuary slab to pay off Fernandez's bills

Outward calm: the home of Delphine Downing and her two-year-old daughter Rainelle in 1949

of Raymond's sister, who unwittingly allowed them to store it in her basement.

There it remained until 15 January, when Raymond returned to collect it. He buried it that night in the basement of a rented house. After Janet's murder the couple cashed her cheques and created the illusion that she was still alive and well by sending cheery letters to her relatives. But these messages only aroused her family's curiosity, because they were all typed. Janet Fay had never learned to use a typewriter.

THE WIDOW AND HER DAUGHTER

Meanwhile, the killer couple had moved on to Grand Rapids, Michigan where Raymond seduced their next victim. Her name was Delphine Downing and she was a 41-year-old widow and mother with whom he had been corresponding under the pen name 'Charles Martin'. Raymond was a quick worker and within weeks courtship had moved on to sex. But one morning Delphine went into the bathroom and caught a glimpse of the real Raymond Fernandez without his toupee. She went into hysterics and accused him of deceit. The screaming roused Martha who persuaded the distraught woman to take a sleeping pill and go back to bed. During all of this commotion Delphine's two-year-old daughter, Rainelle, started to cry, at which point Martha lost control. She throttled the child until she lost consciousness.

Raymond panicked at the thought of Delphine waking up and seeing the girl's bruises, so he went to fetch a gun that had belonged to her husband. When he returned to the bedroom he wrapped a blanket around it to deaden the sound and then he fired one shot at point blank range. Delphine was dead. They buried her in the basement and covered the hole with cement. Then for two days they ransacked the place where she lived, taking everything of value. By that time the little girl had regained consciousness and was crying for her mother. Unable to cope, Martha drowned the toddler in a tub, after which she too was buried in the basement. Then they went to the cinema, but on their return they found two police officers waiting for them. The neighbours had reported hearing a child crying for the past two days and there had been no sign of its mother.

At the Kent County district attorney's office the couple signed a 73-page confession detailing their crimes, in return for an assurance that they would not stand trial in New York, which had the death penalty. Michigan did not. There was an understanding that Raymond would probably be released in six years, although with three murders hanging over him it is almost impossible to believe that he would ever have been allowed to walk free. The press showed the couple no mercy, describing them as degenerates and demanding the death penalty. Nor was there a shred of sympathy from the district attorney's office. The Kent County authorities finally bowed to public pressure and on 8 March 1949 Beck and Fernandez were handed over to the New York prosecutors for trial in relation to the murder of Janet Fay. The shadow of the electric chair loomed ever larger.

THE HOTTEST TICKET IN TOWN

Despite the blistering heat the courtroom was packed when the trial opened on 9 June 1949. The *New York Times* reported that many female spectators gladly skipped their lunch to keep their seats. When the couple's confession was read out aloud during the proceedings it included stories of three-way strip poker, with Raymond as the prize.

THE LITTLE GIRL HAD REGAINED CONSCIOUSNESS AND WAS CRYING FOR HER MOTHER. UNABLE TO COPE, MARTHA DROWNED THE TODDLER IN A TUB, AFTER WHICH SHE TOO WAS BURIED IN THE BASEMENT

On the day that Martha finally took the stand, two dozen extra policemen were called in to hold back the crowds jostling for a place. She described the sordid sex acts she and Raymond had indulged in as part of his voodoo rituals, but she refused to find such activities abnormal.

'We loved each other and I consider it absolutely sacred... You referred to the lovemaking as abnormal but for the love I had for Fernandez, nothing is abnormal!... a request from Mr Fernandez to me is a command. I loved him enough to do anything he asked me to!'

She also said, 'Raymond got quite a kick out of the photographs some of the old hags sent him, expecting to correspond with him.'

But she claimed to have no recollection of the murder of Janet Fay, only of the lifeless body lying at her feet. It was her idea, she said, to wrap a scarf around Mrs Fay's neck, but it had been in an effort to save her, not strangle her. Her training as a nurse had taught her that 'a tourniquet about the neck would stop bleeding from the head'. Her self-deception was staggering.

On 18 August 1949 the jury returned after an all-night sitting. Their verdict was delivered to an empty courtoom. It was 8.30 am and the spectators had not expected such a quick decision. The judge noted the verdict – both defendants were found guilty in the first degree – and he postponed sentencing until 22 August.

On that day Raymond Fernandez and Martha Beck were both sentenced to die in the electric chair at Sing Sing. While they lingered on Death Row Raymond wrote letters of love and longing to his first wife, giving little thought to Martha who agonized over her faithless lover, insulting him one moment and forgiving him the next.

'What do they expect me to do? Sit here and let him destroy the one thread of decency I have left? He has done so much talking about how he has me wrapped around his little finger that it was a blow to his ego when I unwrapped myself and forgot about him... All I can say is: what a character! Oh yes, he's brave when it comes to talk and hurting others – he can kill without batting an eyelash – but to hurt himself – he'd never do it. It takes a man to kill himself. Not a snivelling, low-down, double-crossing, lying rat like him!'

But on the last day of their lives, 8 March 1951, they made up, sending notes between the cell blocks professing eternal affection for each other.

'The news brought to me that Martha loves me is the best I've had in years,' said Raymond. 'Now I'm ready to die! So tonight I'll die like a man!'

But he died a pitiful figure, having to be carried to the death chamber because he was too frightened to walk unaided. His last words were

'RAYMOND GOT QUITE A KICK OUT OF THE PHOTOGRAPHS SOME OF THE OLD HAGS SENT HIM, EXPECTING TO CORRESPOND WITH HIM'

Eternal optimists: Beck and Fernandez flank their attorney, looking as if they still believe he can get them off the hook

delivered in a voice that was broken with emotion.

'I want to shout it out. I love Martha! What do the public know about love?'

Martha's final statement was equally hysterical.

'What does it matter who is to blame? My story is a love story, but only those tortured with love can understand what I mean. I was pictured as a fat unfeeling woman... I am not unfeeling, stupid or moronic... in the history of the world how many crimes have been attributed to love?'

She had difficulty squeezing into the chair as the matrons strapped her down. Then she mouthed her last words.

'So long.'

At 11.24 pm the current surged through her massive frame. Minutes later she was officially pronounced dead.

CHAPTER 2

PARTNERS IN CRIME

Murders committed purely for profit are often the wilful acts of uncommonly callous, self-centred pathological personalities, devoid of conscience and compassion. These individuals are surely the very personification of evil, for they commit their crimes with a complete disregard for the consequences and cannot conceive of their victims as anything other than a commodity to be disposed of at their will.

THE BABY FARM –

LILA AND WILLIAM YOUNG

If the accusations against Canadian 'baby farmers' Lila Gladys and William Peach Young are true, the couple must surely qualify as two of the most heartless killers in history. And yet, against all the odds and in spite of all the evidence accumulated against them, they evaded arrest and prosecution for their crimes.

The daughter of devoutly religious parents, Lila had lived an uneventful life until she met and married William Young, an Oregon-born medical missionary in the Seventh-day Adventist Church. William had failed to qualify as a doctor, but he seemed undeterred by the fact. On the contrary, he was convinced an unshakeable belief in his 'calling' was all he needed to be able to practise medicine on the unfortunate heathens. He could not have

heard the call loud enough, though, because he did not venture further than Nova Scotia, where he and his new bride opened the Ideal Maternity Home and Sanitarium in February 1928 as 'an expectant mothers refuge'. Unwed mothers-to-be and those women seeking discreet births were promised 'no publicity' and somewhere to dispose of their unwanted progeny.

It was an offer that soon brought clients from all over the state. The couple's desperate clients thought the term 'disposal' was a euphemism for the arranging of a discreet adoption, but the Youngs were not humanitarians by nature and they had no intention of spending their fees on the long-term care of the infants in their charge.

Their services and their silence did not, of

UNWED MOTHERS-TO-BE AND WOMEN SEEKING DISCREET BIRTHS WERE PROMISED 'NO PUBLICITY' AND SOMEWHERE TO DISPOSE OF THEIR UNWANTED PROGENY

The Youngs came from deeply religious backgrounds, but they never let that impinge on their money-making activities

course, come cheap. Married women were required to pay $75 for two weeks' stay at the Sanitarium, while single mothers were charged as much as $200, plus $12 for sundry items such as nappies and $2 a week for nursing while the adoption was being arranged. But the most lucrative item was the $20 charge for infant funerals, of which there were many – far more in fact than could possibly be attributed to natural causes. The Youngs paid local handyman Glen Shatford 50 cents to dispatch the babies. He placed the infant in a butterbox obtained from the grocery store before burying it in waste ground. Shatford later confessed to burying up to 125 infants in a field owned by Lila's

unsuspecting parents. Other children were more fortunate. They were farmed out to neighbours, who kept them alive for as long as they could on the mere $3 a week provided by the callous couple. For this long-term bed and board the Youngs charged the mothers $300. Babies of mixed-race parentage and those with disabilities were allegedly starved to death on a diet of water and molasses, presumably in the belief that they were being spared a fate worse than death.

More cost-cutting measures were adopted by the Youngs. Poor girls were given the chance to work off their debt as domestic servants, which cut the costs of their upkeep and ensured that

Deviousness and deceit paid real dividends as the Youngs set themselves up in a 54-room mansion

no outsiders could learn the truth of what was happening at the Sanitarium. Trained medical staff were excluded. Clients were billed for the services of two doctors, but in practice Lila acted as midwife while William knelt at the foot of the bed and prayed for the unfortunate sinner.

The Youngs' deviousness and deceit paid real dividends when it came to the fees they charged prospective parents, who willingly handed over up to $1,000 per child for a no-questions-asked adoption, a fee which had increased to $5,000 by the 1940s. By fleecing their clients at both ends of the baby chain the Youngs were estimated to have netted $3.5 million and by the outbreak of the Second World War they had moved into a 54-room mansion. This large building could house up to 70 infants in its nursery and there were private rooms for wealthier clients who were willing to pay a premium for privacy. And there were always additional 'windfalls' to be had from guilt-ridden young mothers who desperately wanted their babies back after they had changed their minds. The price of retrieval was said to be $10,000.

THINGS FALL APART

By all accounts the bullish Lila saw her charges as a burden and she was brutal in her handling of the women who came under her care. In March 1936 the couple were charged with the manslaughter of a mother and her baby, but after a three-day trial both were acquitted for lack of evidence. It was not until nine years later that public health officials received so many complaints of insanitary conditions and neglect that they could no longer afford to ignore them. The Youngs' application for a licence to operate under the Maternity Boarding House Act of 1940 was turned down while the complaints against them were being investigated and in spring 1945 the United States Department of Immigration threatened to prosecute the couple for smuggling children across the Canadian border into the United States. Additional charges were brought for practising medicine without a licence, for which they were subsequently convicted, but Lila and William walked free after paying a token fine of $150. Another conviction for selling babies across the United States border followed in June, but again a modest fine of less than $500 was imposed and the Youngs returned to their lucrative baby farming business.

GREED AND ARROGANCE

Lila's greed and arrogance were ultimately her undoing. She countered the claims made by a local newspaper with a suit for harassment, but the press were not to be bullied or intimidated as easily as her staff. The newspaper persuaded a number of witnesses to come forward with damning testimony at the hearing, which ensured that the claim for damages was summarily dismissed. Furthermore, the maternity home went out of business before the end of the year. After the Youngs had been exposed they were soon filing for bankruptcy to stave off the deluge of claims that followed. They were also forced to sell their property and move to Quebec.

In 1962 alcoholism and cancer claimed the life of William Young and Lila succumbed to leukaemia five years later. She was buried in a plot close to the unmarked graves of her tiny victims.

> THERE WERE ADDITIONAL WINDFALLS TO BE HAD FROM GUILT-RIDDEN YOUNG MOTHERS WHO WANTED THEIR BABIES BACK AFTER THEY HAD CHANGED THEIR MINDS

THE MONSTER BUTLER AND HIS ACCOMPLICE –

ARCHIBALD HALL AND MICHAEL KITTO

rior to his death in September 2002, Archibald Hall had the unenviable distinction of being the oldest person in Britain serving a life sentence. It was not the honour he had been hoping for.

Hall was born into a working-class district of Glasgow on 17 June 1924, the eldest of three children. By his own admission he had enjoyed a conventional upbringing and had performed well at school. However, he had a passive-aggressive personality that manifested itself in periodic outbursts of violence, the most notable being the

occasion on which he had held a knife to his father's throat in an argument over a jacket. Hall evidently resented his lowly origins and was determined to prove himself the equal of the wealthier residents of the city, whom he secretly envied. He began by reinventing himself as a well-educated, softly-spoken young man, which enabled him to con his way into middle-class households under a variety of pretexts, with a view to pocketing whatever he could. He also bamboozled the local Red Cross into allowing him to act as a collection agent, for which he used two tins – one for small change and the other for larger donations, which he kept for himself.

A sexually precocious youth, he had a voracious appetite for both genders and boasted of having had a series of casual male lovers by the age of 15, as well as an affair with an older woman, who gave him a taste of the lavish lifestyle he hungered after. The discovery that he was bisexual led to his decision to leave Scotland for the bright lights of London, where he thought he might be less conspicuous. There he successfully blended into the gay community, where he passed himself off as a wealthy American. He also ingratiated himself with the upper strata of society, enriching himself in the process. However, his plans did not go as

> **HALL HAD A PASSIVE-AGGRESSIVE PERSONALITY THAT MANIFESTED ITSELF IN PERIODIC OUTBURSTS OF VIOLENCE**

Hall (above) reinvented himself as a well-educated, softly-spoken young man; Kitto was a petty thief

David Wright threatened to expose Hall, ensuring a big surprise when he went down to the woods one day...

smoothly as he had hoped. Shortly after moving south he was caught attempting to sell stolen jewellery and was given a stiff prison sentence. But his incarceration provided him with a unique opportunity to spend hours in the prison library, where he researched the subjects that would prove profitable in the profession he planned to pursue on his release – that of butler to the rich and famous. While the other inmates paced their cells or stared at the walls, Hall read everything he could on the subject of antiques and etiquette.

A 'GENTLEMAN'S GENTLEMAN'

On his release he adopted the name Roy Fontaine and found a position as a 'gentleman's gentleman'

to a member of the English aristocracy, which gave him ample opportunity to make an inventory of the silverware and other valuables. Hall's greatest assets were his dapper appearance and his carefully cultivated air of respectability, which immediately put prospective employers at their ease. He simply looked and acted the part to perfection. He was also acutely aware of how much store the aristocracy set by servants who knew their place, and so he was suitably deferential. This gave his victims the impression that he could be trusted. But beneath his veneer of cordiality Hall had no respect for the upper classes and his crimes could be seen as his way of making them pay for what he perceived as their arrogance.

Hall was a hedonist, a power-seeker who was driven by a need to avenge himself on a society from which he believed himself to be excluded. He was not a typical serial killer, but he was a psychopath. If his own story is to be believed, he had no history of having suffered abuse at home or at school, where he had earned good grades. He had not exhibited any tell-tale traits such as cruelty towards animals, nor had he drawn attention to himself through aberrant behaviour. It was simply that he was an opportunist thief who would kill to cover his tracks because he was desperate to avoid being exposed as a criminal. Such a situation would have been entirely at odds with his own self-image of socialite and consummate actor. But although he was a convincing conman he was not a lucky one and before long he had once again been detained at Her Majesty's Pleasure, having been caught red-handed selling stolen property.

He returned to Scotland after his release in 1975 and despite his criminal record he managed to find work as a butler to Lady Hudson in Dumfriesshire. His intention had been to rob her, too, but he realized that he liked the dowager and his duties too much to risk losing them and he seriously considered 'going straight'. All might have ended well for Hall at this point, but unfortunately a former male lover and cell mate, David Wright, had obtained a job on the same estate. He threatened to expose Hall to his employer if he dared prevent him from helping himself to the old lady's jewels. Hall's solution was to lure Wright into the woods on the pretext of making him an offer to buy his silence and then shoot him in the back of the head with a gun used for hunting rabbits.

But Hall knew that even his silver tongue would not be able to convince the police that it had been a hunting accident, so he buried the body and submitted his resignation before he could be summarily dismissed.

His next job took him back to London where he used Lady Hudson's name to secure the position of head butler to the elderly Walter Scott-Elliot, a former Labour Member of Parliament, and his wife Dorothy.

A FATAL PARTNERSHIP

Hall took the first opportunity to bring his lover and accomplice Mary Coggles into the household as a cleaner. She in turn introduced Hall to petty thief Michael Kitto, who proved the perfect foil for the avaricious conman. Kitto was a subservient, colourless individual whose fawning admiration

> HALL'S SOLUTION WAS TO LURE WRIGHT INTO THE WOODS ON THE PRETEXT OF MAKING HIM AN OFFER TO BUY HIS SILENCE AND THEN SHOOT HIM IN THE BACK OF THE HEAD WITH A GUN USED FOR HUNTING RABBITS

for Hall's schemes fed his warped ego. Together the trio planned the robbery they hoped would set them up for life. But Mrs Scott-Elliot returned home early and demanded to know why her butler was showing a stranger around her home. Before Hall could offer an explanation Kitto had subdued the old lady by smothering her with a pillow.

Hall was just a career conman with convictions for nothing more serious than burglary and the chances were that Wright's murder would have remained undetected. However, he had made the fatal mistake of falling in with an unstable homicidal criminal who had now embroiled him in a second killing.

As they struggled to put the body to bed in an effort to make it appear that the woman had died in her sleep, her elderly husband awoke. Hall, however, kept his head and reassured the old man that all was well. Mrs Scott-Elliot had suffered a nightmare and he was putting her back to bed, so the old man could go back to sleep. The next morning Hall and Kitto cooked up a plot. They would sedate the husband and then drive up to Cumberland, where Hall had rented a holiday cottage. On the way, they would dispose of Mrs Scott-Elliot's body, which would be bundled into the boot. Mary Coggles would be persuaded to sit next to the old man, wearing his wife's wig and fur coat, for the benefit of any witnesses.

With that accomplished, Hall and Kitto returned to the scene of the crime and ransacked the house before travelling north again, where they tried to finish off the husband by strangling him. But he fought hard for his life so they beat him to death with a shovel and buried him at another remote location.

DANGEROUS LIABILITY

By this point Mary Coggles had become a dangerous liability. She had insisted on keeping the murdered woman's jewellery and furs and had boasted to friends of her part in the affair. So Hall killed her too, caving in her skull with a poker and suffocating her with a plastic bag, before dumping her body under a bridge. The discovery of her corpse on Christmas Day 1977 did not, however, lead to the capture of the odd couple. It was the killing of their next victim, Hall's step-brother Donald, that was their undoing.

Donald was a paedophile who had recently been released from prison. Having nowhere else to go, he invited himself to his brother's holiday home in Cumbria. He asked too many awkward questions, though, so Archibald and Kitto rendered him senseless with chloroform and then drowned him in the bath. But instead of burying him nearby Hall and Kitto decided to take the body to Scotland in the boot of their car and then dispose of it. It was

DONALD ASKED TOO MANY QUESTIONS AND WAS RENDERED SENSELESS WITH CHLOROFORM, THEN DROWNED IN THE BATH

Non-silent partner: Mary Coggles couldn't keep her mouth shut, so Hall caved her skull in with a poker

an unnecessary risk and one which cost them their freedom. Before they reached their destination the weather worsened and they were forced to stay overnight at a hotel in North Berwick, where the landlord's suspicions were aroused by their odd behaviour. He was worried that the pair might try to leave the next day without paying their bill, so he decided to call the police who checked the numberplates on their car.

When they were found to be false, two uniformed bobbies were dispatched to the hotel. The car was searched and the body was found in the boot. Hall and Kitto were immediately arrested, but Hall managed to escape through a bathroom window during a break in the interrogation. He was soon recaptured in a nearby town.

The two men were tried twice – once in England and once in Scotland – for the five murders. Hall was found guilty of four of them, with the killing of Mrs Scott-Elliot set aside for legal reasons, while Kitto was convicted of three murders and sentenced to serve a minimum of 15 years.

The English judge told Hall that there was no possibility he would ever be released. With no hope whatsoever of freedom, he attempted suicide on several occasions but was unsuccessful. In 1999 he published his autobiography and called it *A Perfect Gentleman*, presumably with irony rather than in earnest.

A STITCH IN CRIME –

RAY AND FAYE COPELAND

Murderers invariably have a motive. Some kill in cold blood for profit, or for sexual or sadistic satisfaction. Others kill in the heat of passion – they might be avenging an imagined insult or trying to prevent a former lover from leaving them. Many commit murder to conceal a crime. A few might even believe that they are carrying out a mercy killing to end the suffering of another, or that they have been chosen by a vengeful God to kill in his name.

Nebraska couple Ray and Faye Copeland might have been unique in that they murdered complete strangers because they simply could not think of another way of life. Ray is thought to have murdered as many as 12 vagrants and runaways during the 1970s and 1980s, after they had served

their purpose in his fraudulent livestock deals, while his wife Faye kept silent. A dull, callous man, he saw the men's deaths as akin to killing a stray dog. He took no particular pleasure in it but he did not give it a second thought either, while his wife maintained that it was not her business to criticize her husband.

'I was raised to love my husband and support him no matter what,' she later said. 'The man is the head of the family. The Bible says it should be that way... Maybe we'd have got along better if I had knocked the sh*t out of him a few times.'

In August 1989 a 57-year-old farm labourer named Jack McCormick contacted the Nebraska police with an incredible story about a farmer who had tried to kill him back in Missouri. It was

> THE COPELANDS MURDERED COMPLETE STRANGERS BECAUSE THEY SIMPLY COULD NOT THINK OF ANOTHER WAY OF LIFE

Murder on their minds: the Copelands looked like any old-fashioned farming couple but they killed again and again

after McCormick had stumbled upon the farmer's scheme to buy livestock with worthless cheques signed by drifters and vagrants like himself. But that was not all. Before he ran for his life, McCormick had unearthed human bones on his employer's land, which made him suspect that other farm workers might not have been as lucky as he had been.

The Missouri authorities might have dismissed the claims as the mischievous act of a disgruntled employee had it not been for the fact that the farmer had been under suspicion for some time.

Copeland, 76 years old at the time, had a thick file for theft and fraud going back a long way, but he had evaded arrest by pointing to the fact that the signatures on the worthless cheques were not his. He had been seen in the company of the murdered drifters on the day of the cattle market and had been giving them the nod as to what and when to buy, but the men could not be traced when the cheques they had signed were returned unpaid by the bank.

The local sheriff decided that he needed to unearth the evidence before Copeland could destroy it. So early on the morning of 9 October 1989, Sheriff Leland O'Dell arrived on Copeland's land with 40 officers and dozens of bloodhounds. They began searching the property.

THE GRISLY QUILT

The investigators spent a fruitless week scouring the acres of farmland but eventually their thoroughness paid off. Three bodies were found in shallow graves in a barn that stood on an adjacent plot. All three were young males who had been shot once in the back of the head. They were later identified as Paul Cowart, from Arkansas, John Freeman, from Oklahoma, and Jimmie Harvey, from Missouri.

A fourth body, that of Wayne Warner, was found wrapped in plastic sheeting under the floor of a barn at another location and a fifth was discovered nearby. It was that of Dennis Murphy.

The last two men had also been killed by a bullet in the back of the head. Ballistic tests subsequently identified Ray Copeland's .22 calibre rifle as the murder weapon. Copeland's wife Faye was also indicted because detectives had found a list of 12 names in her handwriting, all with an 'X' by the side. All of the named men were missing persons and five of them were linked with the bodies found at the farm. It was later discovered that Faye Copeland had used material from the men's clothing to make a quilt.

The police were anxious to trace the other missing men so they offered Faye a deal, but she refused to co-operate, insisting that she had no knowledge of the killings. At her trial in November 1990 she claimed that she had not attempted to stop her husband's homicidal activities because she was a battered wife and in fear of her life. But the incriminating list she had made, together with the quilt, convinced the jury that she was an accomplice to first degree murder. The judge sentenced her to death by lethal injection. When Ray was asked by the sheriff for his reaction his muttered response was terse.

'Well, those things happen to some, you know.'

Ray Copeland's trial began six months later, following a thorough assessment of his mental health. With no grounds to support an insanity plea his defence was hopeless and he was convicted on all counts and sentenced to death. Two years later the 78-year-old suffered a fatal heart attack while he awaited execution, so he took the location of the other victims to the grave with him.

On 6 August 1999 the death sentence imposed upon 78-year-old Faye Copeland was commuted to life imprisonment. Three years later she had a stroke and was permitted to leave the prison for a nursing home where she died in December 2003 aged 82. At one of the later hearings for clemency she restated her innocence.

'God will forgive me for anything I've said or done.'

A MARRIAGE MADE IN HELL —

JAMES MARLOW
AND CYNTHIA COFFMAN

As the privileged daughter of a St Louis businessman, Cynthia Coffman enjoyed the good life, but she was forced into a loveless marriage when she became pregnant at the age of 17.

Her devoutly Catholic parents refused to let her have an abortion and they threatened to cut her off without a cent if she did not marry before the neighbours noticed her condition. But after five years of domestic tedium Cynthia left her husband and young son to hit the highway. She had no plans, other than to get as far away as she could from the life she loathed. When she ran out of fuel and options in Page, Arizona she did what all unqualified young women in smalltown America would do — she took a job as a waitress in a diner. She then met a local man and moved into his apartment, but they were evicted shortly afterwards when the neighbours complained about their drunken behaviour.

In May 1986 the couple were arrested for speeding during a road trip to California and Cynthia's boyfriend was jailed for six weeks for possessing an unlicensed gun. It was while she was visiting him in prison that Cynthia set eyes on her boyfriend's cell mate — bad boy James Gregory Marlow — and decided that she wanted to

Coffman left her life of privilege and ended up with Marlow

The body of 19-year-old Lynel Murray was discovered in a Huntington Beach motel room; there was evidence of sexual assault

change partners. Marlow, who was 29 years old, had convictions for robbery with violence, burglary and car theft. He also had delusions of his own superiority and wore tattoos of the neo-Nazi Aryan Brotherhood with pride.

'I BELONG TO THE FOLSOM WOLF'

Cynthia was not there to meet her boyfriend when he was finally released from jail. She and Marlow were on their way south to fleece Marlow's family of all they could beg, borrow or steal. It was not long before his relatives got wise to them and sent them packing, forcing the couple to sleep rough in the woods, where they doused themselves with petrol to keep the ticks off. Within days Marlow was back to breaking into houses and making off with petty cash and any weapons he could lay his hands on. That July they were married. The nuptials were sealed in an unusual way, with the bride having her buttocks tattooed with the inscription, 'I belong to the Folsom Wolf'.

But that autumn their criminal careers took a

nasty turn when they kidnapped and murdered 32-year-old Sandra Neary in Costa Mesa, California. Sandra's car was found abandoned in a local car park, where she had gone to withdraw money from a cash machine. Two weeks later her body was found in Riverside County. She had been strangled.

The couple's next target was 35-year-old Pamela Simmons, who disappeared on 28 October in Bullhead City. She too had been abducted while withdrawing money from a cash machine and her vehicle was also found abandoned nearby. A third girl was kidnapped and killed just ten days later in Redlands. 20-year-old Corinna Novis had been taken from a shopping mall in broad daylight.

The fourth person to be murdered was 19-year-old psychology student Lynel Murray. Her boyfriend reported her missing on 12 November after she had missed a date. He found her car parked outside the dry-cleaning shop in Orange County where she worked and contacted the police. The following day her body was discovered in a Huntington Beach motel room. She was naked and there was evidence of sexual assault. At this point the police were sure they were looking for a serial killer because an almost identical method had been employed in each of the four slayings, but they had no inkling that a woman was involved or that the crimes had been committed by a couple.

But then they got lucky.

THE KILLERS LEFT THEIR NAMES BEHIND

A chequebook belonging to Corinna Novis was found in a dumpster at Laguna Niguel. It was stuffed into a fast food bag that also contained a bill with the names of the customers on it – Cynthia and James Marlow. The same day the police were called to a San Bernardino motel where the couple had stayed. They had passed the time practising Lynel Murray's signature on motel stationery and left this evidence behind them. A nationwide search was initiated, which led to a tip-off from the owner of a mountain lodge at Big Bear City, California. A huge police contingent surrounded the lodge but the occupants had fled. They were spotted a few hours later on a mountain pass, where they were apprehended without a struggle.

Whatever alibis they might have rehearsed fell apart when the police pointed out to them that they were both wearing clothes known to have been stolen from the dry cleaners where victim Lynel Murray had worked.

Cynthia confessed and then offered to show the detectives where they had buried the body

Marlow and Coffman got careless when they left a bill with their names on it in a bag containing a victim's chequebook

of Corinna Novis, who had been sodomized and strangled. The forensic evidence against the couple was compelling. Their fingerprints were recovered from Corinna's car and Cynthia was identified by the owner of the pawnshop where she had sold the dead woman's typewriter.

On 17 November 1986 the pair were formally charged with the murders. As the date for the trial approached the recriminations began. By the time they took the stand their enmity was raw, each blaming the other for their fate. When she was asked if she needed anything, Cynthia told her lawyer that all she wanted was some way of erasing the tattoo from her buttocks. Then on 30 August 1989 a guilty verdict was returned for both parties on all counts and the sentence of death was recorded.

An appeal for a retrial was made to the California Supreme Court, on the grounds that the couple should have been tried separately, but in August 2004 the petition was rejected. Justice Kathryn M. Werdegar concluded that there was sufficient independent evidence against both defendants and that an abuse of discretion had not denied them separate trials. The case against them was so strong that any error in not ordering a separate trial would have been 'harmless beyond a reasonable doubt'.

Justice Werdegar rejected Cynthia's claim that she had only acted as an accomplice because Marlow had beaten her and threatened to harm her six-year-old son and she dismissed Marlow's attempts to blame Cynthia for the California killings. Marlow had testified that it had been Cynthia's idea to kill Corinna Novis, whereas he had only intended to rob her, but witnesses – including

Coffman's cell mate – had confirmed that each of the accused had taken credit for the murder.

The judge also rebuffed Coffman's contention that she should not be executed because she was less culpable than Marlow.

'... Coffman, 24 years old at the time of the offenses, was found by the jury to have committed murder and to have engaged in the charged felonies with the intent to kill or to aid or abet Marlow in killing the victim. The jury also heard evidence that Coffman, together with Marlow, had committed another similar murder and other felony offenses in Orange County. Evidently the jury was not persuaded that Coffman suffered from such physical abuse or emotional or psychological oppression as to warrant a sentence less than death. Contrary to Coffman's argument, the offenses here were of the most serious nature, and her sentence clearly befits her personal culpability.'

CYNTHIA CONFESSED AND THEN OFFERED TO SHOW THE DETECTIVES WHERE THEY HAD BURIED THE BODY

ANGELS WITHOUT MERCY

GWENDOLYN GRAHAM AND CATHERINE WOOD

It is a sad and sobering fact that not all nurses and doctors are caring and compassionate professionals who put the wellbeing of their patients first. Michigan nurses Gwendolyn Gail Graham, 23, and Catherine May Wood, 24, might have been qualified to care for the elderly but they were certainly not compassionate or caring by nature. Quite the opposite, in fact.

The two women first met at the Alpine Manor Nursing Home in Walker, Michigan in 1987 where Wood was employed as a head nurse and Graham as her assistant. They became lesbian lovers and practised asphyxia to heighten their sexual pleasure. One thing led to another and before long they were discussing strangling their patients for kicks, going so far as to choose victims whose initials would spell out M-U-R-D-E-R, just in case the police were too slow to catch on. But the elderly women Graham chose for her first victims put up such a struggle that she had to give up. Incredibly none of her intended victims alerted the other staff or accused Graham of assault.

Graham then chose a victim who would not fight back. She was a patient with Alzheimer's disease who was smothered to death with little effort, while Wood kept a lookout. The next victims were easy to dispatch too. Wood stood guard outside

Gwen Graham (top) and Cathy Wood were lesbian lovers who got their kicks by taking the lives of helpless victims

their rooms, while Graham suffocated them with a washcloth. Money was not the prime motive, even though the helpless women were robbed of their jewellery – the pair were sexually aroused by killing. They frequently slipped into an empty bedroom to satiate their lust as they relived the grisly details.

While they were there they fingered the souvenirs they had stolen from the crime scene. They did not just take jewellery and other valuables. Often it was mundane items, such as the victim's dentures. More appalling was the revelation that they even experienced sexual stimulation while preparing the bodies in the mortuary.

Yet no one employed at the nursing home suspected that the pair were acting oddly. Even when they boasted of what they were doing, their confessions were dismissed as a sick joke.

All the while Wood had been the passive partner, acting as lookout while Graham did the grisly deed, but then Graham demanded that Wood take a turn. She refused, transferring to another shift to avoid being taunted by her former lover. Graham,

however, was insatiable. She found another lesbian partner and then took a job in a hospital maternity unit in Texas. Wood broke down and confessed all to her ex-husband when she heard that Graham had threatened to kill one of the babies, but he would not believe her.

He refused to go to the police. It was not until a year later that he finally relented, at which point the terrible truth came to light.

Graham and Wood played their so-called 'murder game' for about three months, during which time it is thought that they murdered as many as 40 elderly patients, though they were initially charged with killing five. Wood bargained for a lenient sentence by turning state's evidence, laying all the blame on her dominant, sadistic former partner. Graham's defence counsel countered that Wood had invented the whole story in order to avenge herself on Graham for taking a new lover, but the jury was not buying it. Graham was convicted of first degree murder in all five cases and one count of conspiracy to commit murder, for which she received six concurrent life sentences, with no possibility of parole.

KILL OR CURE: PSYCHOPATHIC NURSES

The public is naturally shocked and mystified whenever it hears about care workers killing their patients, but sadly such cases are not as rare as we might expect. This aberrant behaviour can be explained in various ways.

Some employees simply seek attention or notoriety. These individuals have low self-esteem, so even negative attention is better than being ignored and taken for granted. If they did not kill for financial gain, others might offer the defence that they are suffering from a personality disorder known as Munchausen By Proxy Syndrome (in which a person deliberately brings about illness or injury in others in order to gain a benefit, such as attention). However, it could be argued that anyone who commits a wilful act of murder is not entirely in their right mind, because murder itself is an act of temporary insanity. Those who genuinely suffer from the disorder will deliberately endanger the lives of those in their care in order to create a situation where only they can save them. This satisfies the illusion that they are indispensable to the patient and the institution. Endangering the lives of the patients will give them a sense of superiority over the doctors and other medical staff, whose knowledge and experience makes them feel inferior. Others relish the power they have been given over life and death and if they feel protected by the institution they work for – believing it might ignore the evidence for fear of a scandal – they will exploit that situation to see how much they can get away with.

The fact that many of those convicted of killing vulnerable patients express no remorse is indicative of a psychopathic personality. These individuals are simply angry at the world for whatever reason and have decided to take out their rage and resentment on those who are least likely to fight back.

MOTHER AND SON OF ALL CONFIDENCE TRICKSTERS –
SANTE AND KENNY KIMES

Professional conmen generally fall into two specific categories – those who are only in it for the money and those who get a thrill from fooling the gullible. Those in the second category are often smart and they are aware of their limitations. They also know when they are pushing their luck and they have the sense to pull out before they are caught. By contrast, those who operate a confidence trick only for the money often become ensnared in their own web of deception and can resort to murder to cover their tracks.

Sante Louise Kimes and her son Kenny fell into the first category. Their greed was so great that they resorted to murder even though their rackets had already made them wealthy beyond their dreams. Sante (born Sante Singhrs in Oklahoma City) was of Dutch–East Indian parentage. She delighted in the fact that she bore a passing resemblance to the Hollywood star Elizabeth Taylor and would impersonate the celebrity whenever she could gain an advantage by doing so.

By the time she had married her second husband, motel tycoon Kenneth Kimes, she had amassed a small fortune from fraud, forgery and making false insurance claims for property that she had burned to the ground. Not content to be merely wealthy, she hungered for esteem and admiration, which led her to gatecrash a White House reception during President Ford's residency by introducing her husband as an ambassador.

But Sante's elegance and charm was a facade that hid a cruel and exploitative nature. She enslaved young illegal immigrants and threatened to have them deported if they disobeyed her. But it was impossible to keep their existence a secret for long in modern America. When the United States immigration authorities learned of the conditions in which she kept her servants they arrested her and took her to court. In August 1985 she ended up with a five-year prison sentence. Four years later she was free and up to her old tricks, although this time she was burning with resentment. She was determined to make society pay for the time she had languished in prison, out of the spotlight.

KENNY JOINS THE TEAM

When her husband died in 1994, Sante introduced her son Kenny to the con game. He was a quick learner. The pair are believed to have been behind the murder of Mississippi heiress Jacqueline Levitz, who mysteriously disappeared in 1995 and was declared dead in 2001. It is thought that Sante and Kenny had hoped to claim the Levitz estate, but when that failed they cast their net wider.

Oedipal killers: Sante and Kenny Kimes made a fortune, but wanted more and more... they couldn't stop themselves

When Sante was refused a loan by a suspicious Indian banker, Syed Bilal Ahmed, in September 1996 they killed him by drugging him and drowning him in the bath at his home in the Bahamas. The next morning they dumped him in the sea. Back in New York in 1998, Sante and her son ingratiated themselves into the home of the millionairess Irene Silverman, who mysteriously vanished soon afterwards. Although her body was never found, the deadly duo were tried and found guilty of her murder and of attempting to steal her Manhattan mansion. Not only had they had been stupid enough to write their plans down, but they had also been condemned by the missing woman herself, who had confided her suspicions to her diaries.

Then the lives of mother and son really began to unravel. During a court appearance Kenny went berserk. Armed only with a ballpoint pen he took a reporter hostage. After he was overwhelmed and the hostage released, he and his mother were sent to Los Angeles to answer charges relating to the murder of businessman David Kazdin. They were accused of having killed Kazdin because he had discovered that they had forged his signature in order to obtain a loan that he had not agreed to.

With the threat of the death penalty hanging over him, Kenny changed his plea. He admitted his part in the killing and he also confessed to the earlier murder of the Indian banker, both of which actions he blamed on his mother. Both mother and son are currently serving multiple life sentences with no prospect of parole, having fallen for their own scam – they conned themselves into believing that they could get away with murder.

CHAPTER 3

THE THRILL
OF THE KILL

The following cases are offered to substantiate the claim that criminality is a form of insanity. Motiveless murder is surely proof that these cold-blooded predators have a psychological 'screw loose', some aberration within their brain which distances them from 'right thinking' people who know the difference between 'right' and 'wrong' and have a degree of empathy for their fellow human beings.

A HATE AS HARD AS IRON —

CHARLES STARKWEATHER AND CARIL ANN FUGATE

The killer couples whose murder sprees are depicted in the cult films *Badlands*, *True Romance* and *Natural Born Killers* all have their origins in the murderous rampage embarked on by real-life outlaws Charles Raymond Starkweather and Caril Ann Fugate, who were responsible for a series of random slayings in Nebraska in 1958. The two sociopaths saw themselves as a latter-day Bonnie and Clyde, archetypal teenage antiheroes whose only hope lay in notoriety and eventual self-destruction.

Caril Ann Fugate was just 14 when she fell under the spell of 19-year-old Charles Starkweather, a garbage collector in her middle-class neighbourhood, who proudly boasted that he burned with a hatred that could only be satisfied by killing. It was no idle threat, he assured her. He had a loaded gun and nothing to lose. As a child he had been bullied by the local boys, who had made fun of his short-sightedness and speech impediment until frustration and resentment consumed him with what he called 'a hate as hard as iron'.

Caril Ann was an impressionable girl who hungered for affection and dreamt of being shown the wild side of life by a boy with the looks and attitude of James Dean. So when Starkweather told her that he modelled himself on the doomed film star it was almost inevitable that she would be impressed. And when he complained of periodic headaches and disorientation, the result of a head injury sustained at his previous job, she persuaded herself that she was the only one who could help

STARKWEATHER PROUDLY BOASTED THAT HE BURNED WITH A HATRED THAT COULD ONLY BE SATISFIED BY KILLING. HE HAD A LOADED GUN AND NOTHING TO LOSE

Fugate was an impressionable girl who hungered for affection; Starkweather had the looks and attitude of James Dean

him. They soon became lovers and were seen everywhere together.

Her family was fiercely opposed to their relationship and not only on account of her age. Starkweather never went anywhere without a weapon and Caril Ann's parents were horrified to hear that he had been teaching her how to throw knives. Had they known what he was capable of they would have forbidden her to see him, but they assumed that he was just another moody youth. They hoped that their daughter would soon tire of him once she realized that he could not afford to give her the standard of living she was accustomed to. But Caril Ann's boyfriend was not just another teenage rebel without a cause. He was a sociopath who could not be reasoned with or rehabilitated – only restrained. He was a nasty piece of work, but she was infatuated with him, which made

Robert Jensen and girlfriend Carol King who made a fatal error when they picked up Starkweather and Fugate

her the perfect audience for his murderous rage.

ORPHANED BY HER LOVER

On 1 December 1957 Starkweather finally snapped. He abducted a gas station cashier in Lincoln at the point of a gun and killed him with one shot to the head, execution style. There were no witnesses so he felt safe in confessing the robbery to Caril Ann, though he claimed to have netted more than the $100 he had actually stolen. And he omitted to tell her that he had murdered the 21-year-old cashier.

But the money had run out by 21 January 1958 and Starkweather was evicted from his apartment when he could not afford to pay the rent. In a rage, he stormed off to Caril Ann's house and became embroiled in a violent altercation with her mother, Velda. She slapped him round the face and he retaliated by shooting her dead on the spot. Then he killed her husband with a knife and a bullet to the brain. When the couple's two-year-old daughter started crying he killed her too, slashing her throat and then splitting her skull with his rifle butt.

It is not clear if Caril Ann was present or if she only viewed the carnage after returning from school, but whether she was a witness or not she made no effort to raise the alarm or escape. In fact, she had several opportunities to run away in the ensuing days, but she did not take them. After hiding the bodies in an outbuilding they posted a sign on the door to deter visitors – 'Stay a Way Every Body is Sick With the Flue'. The couple remained alone in the house for the next six days. Occasional callers were palmed off by Caril Ann, who warned them that it would endanger her mother's health if she allowed anyone inside.

By the time suspicious neighbours had worked up enough courage to venture into the house without permission, the young couple had headed off to Bennett, a town 16 miles to the south, where they hoped to find shelter with an old friend of the Fugate family.

But Starkweather was by now in a volatile mental state and anything was likely to trigger another explosive rage. When August Meyer, the 70-year-old farmer with whom they were staying, made a casual remark that was not to the boy's liking, he shot the old man and his dog.

Abandoning their car, which had become stuck in the mud in Meyer's field, the two teenage fugitives walked to the highway and hitched a ride. The unfortunate occupants of the car were Robert Jensen and his girlfriend Carol King, whom he robbed of $4. Starkweather then forced Jensen to drive to an abandoned school where he shot the 17-year-old six times in the back of the head. Jensen's girlfriend Carol King was murdered and mutilated after Starkweather had tried and failed to rape her. When he was later interrogated by police, the young psycho blamed Caril Ann for the vicious attack on Carol King and claimed that he had only shot her boyfriend in self-defence.

Starkweather and Caril Ann then stole the dead couple's car and drove back to Lincoln.

There, on 30 January, they forced their way into the home of banker C. Lauer Ward and stabbed his wife and his maid to death. While he was waiting for Mr Ward, the demented Starkweather broke the neck of the family dog just for fun. When Ward finally walked through the front door he was confronted by Starkweather and there was a struggle for the gun. Ward was pushed down the cellar steps and shot to death. Starkweather and his adoring accomplice then fled the scene in the murdered man's Packard, which they filled with stolen items from the house.

THE FINAL CHASE

By the time they had reached the outskirts of Douglas, Wyoming on 1 February, a state-wide search had been organized and roadblocks were in place. So they decided to switch cars, murdering the new car's owner, salesman Merle Collison. Starkweather later claimed that he had only killed Mr Collison in self-defence, but he had fired nine bullets into the unarmed man, who had been peacefully asleep by the roadside in his Buick. But this time a passing motorist spotted the youth carrying the corpse from the car. After stopping his vehicle and running across the road he fought with Starkweather until a Highway Patrol car drew up and the officer got out to investigate. At that moment Caril Ann panicked and rushed towards the policeman.

'He killed a man!' she shouted.

Starkweather struggled free, abandoned the Buick and fled in the Packard he had stolen from Mr Ward. During the ensuing chase the vehicles raced along at up to 120 mph, but there was no escape for the teenage fugitive. As he approached a road block a squad of National Guard riflemen sprayed the oncoming car with a withering volley of bullets, which forced Starkweather off the road and into a ditch. By the time he had recovered his senses he was surrounded.

There was no point in denying his crimes, although he tried to blame Caril Ann for some of the killings. She remained faithful to her boyfriend, though, despite what she had witnessed.

WHILE HE WAS WAITING FOR MR WARD, THE DEMENTED STARKWEATHER BROKE THE NECK OF THE FAMILY DOG JUST FOR FUN

HIGHWAY TO HELL –
KENNETH AND IRENE DUDLEY

Bad parents: the Dudleys wrapped the bodies of Norman and Charles together before consigning them to the icy depths

I f evidence is needed to support the assertion that killing others is a form of insanity, then one need look no further than the case of itinerant carnival workers Kenneth and Irene Adelle Dudley, who allowed six of their children to die of malnutrition and neglect and then drove across the southern states, dumping the bodies along the route.

According to the confession drawn out of Irene Dudley, her husband was a cruel and vindictive man who starved and brutalized his children in an attempt to teach them discipline. He slapped one of his girls for 'moving a lot', and stuck four fingers down another child's throat for 'hollering'.

Irene denied she had taken part in the abuse and claimed she had secretly fed the children whenever she could. However, the fact that she had given birth to so many children while knowing of her husband's cruelty suggested she condoned his behaviour. And the fact that she had made no attempt to leave him and take the children with her, or even complain to the authorities, made her an accessory in the eyes of the law. Her pleas of innocence following her indictment for murder fell on stony ground. The evidence of her willing participation in the deaths – and disposal – of six of her ten children was overwhelming.

FATAL NEGLECT

The sad and tragic story of the Dudley children unravelled on 9 February 1961, when the first corpse was spotted on Route 1, near Lawrenceville, Virginia. When the young female victim was taken to the local mortuary the medical examiner found evidence of abuse – specifically bruises, broken bones and open sores. The official cause of death, however, was malnutrition and exposure, suggesting that the child had been left to die at the side of the highway in the biting winter winds.

Kenneth and Irene Dudley were itinerant carnival workers

A couple had been questioned at the same spot by a Highway Patrol officer three days earlier, so the local law enforcement authorities immediately responded with a warrant for their detention. The officer had become suspicious when he had seen their battered sedan parked at the roadside and he had been concerned by the poor physical appearance of the children. On the following day the Dudleys were arrested near Fuqua, North Carolina and brought in to Brunswick County jail, where they were questioned at length. At the same time officers traced the couple's two eldest married daughters to addresses in New York. Those interviews revealed that the couple had begun their journey three years earlier in July 1958, with six children in tow. By the time of their arrest, only two-year-old Christine had survived.

Retracing the couple's epic trek across the southern United States in search of work, detectives were able to piece together the terrible events body by body. Four-year-old Claude had been the first to succumb. His body had been wrapped in a blanket and left at Lakeland, Florida on 19 November 1958. Just over a year later, on New Year's Day 1960, the lifeless bodies of ten-year-old Norman and his eight-year-old brother Charles were found floating in Lake Pontchartrain, Louisiana. They had been wrapped in a blanket and tied together before being thrown off a bridge like a sack of garbage. Toddler Deborrah Jane was dispatched in a cardboard box and left on a rubbish heap in Kentucky on 21 May 1960, followed by her nine-year-old sister Carol Ann, who was left by the roadside in freezing temperatures near Lawrenceville on 9 February 1961.

As the details of the family history were unearthed a file on another child was brought to the attention of the detectives. Created in Syracuse, New York in 1946, this record described how Kenneth Dudley had served a term of imprisonment for improper burial. Although no evidence could be produced to support a prosecution for murder, there was overwhelming evidence of cruelty and neglect of such magnitude that it had led directly to the deaths of all six children.

Irene gave a statement to the police. 'Because we had no money at times the children were denied food, as punishment for misbehaviour. At times, my husband and I ate while the children had nothing. We were better off than the children.'

The couple underwent psychiatric evaluation before receiving lengthy jail sentences for treating their children with so much cruelty.

STIR CRAZY —

MYRON LANCE AND WALTER KELBACH

It is a depressing but undeniable fact that some criminals are beyond rehabilitation. Even after their conviction they exhibit no signs of remorse and may even revel in their notoriety and the power of life and death they held over their victims. Sadistic sex killers Walter Kelbach, 28, and Myron Lance, 25, are just two examples of offenders whose release even the most liberal prison reformer would not support.

Both men were ex-convicts and drug addicts. They were also predatory homosexuals with a strong sadistic streak. In December 1966, when their law-abiding neighbours in Salt Lake City were preparing to celebrate Christmas, Kelbach and Lance were high on something other than the festive spirit. They swallowed a potent cocktail of pills and alcohol and then drove to a petrol station, where they robbed the 18-year-old attendant, Stephen Shea, of $147. Then they forced him into their car and drove to a deserted spot, where they raped and killed him. After the pair had argued over who would have the pleasure of murdering the boy they finally decided to settle the matter by tossing a coin. Kelbach, the 'winner', stabbed Shea five times in the chest with a stiletto.

The following day Lance demanded a re-match, so the pair drove to another filling station, where they abducted the attendant Michael Holtz. Again the victim was sodomized by both men before being left to writhe in agony on the ground while they flipped a coin to decide who would kill him. Lance went on to stab Holtz through the heart.

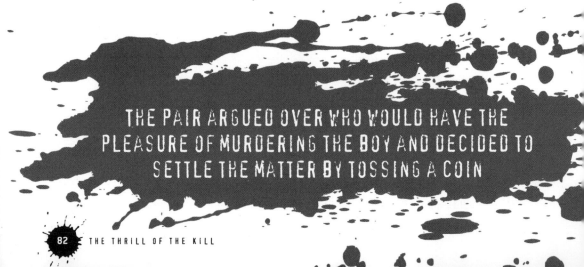

THE PAIR ARGUED OVER WHO WOULD HAVE THE PLEASURE OF MURDERING THE BOY AND DECIDED TO SETTLE THE MATTER BY TOSSING A COIN

Lance (left) and Kelbach were sadistic sex killers who between them didn't possess a single iota of pity for their victims

On 21 December Lance and Kelbach targeted taxi driver Grant Strong. Sensing there was something untoward about his two passengers, Strong pulled over to report his suspicions to his supervisor. It was agreed that he would flip the switch of his radio transmitter if he was in trouble, which he did just moments after driving on.

Kelbach then put a gun to the driver's head and demanded money, but after he had grabbed the night's takings he shot Strong anyway. 'Blood flew everywhere,' Kelbach grinned, recalling the scene. 'Oh boy! I never seen so much blood!' The police arrived too late to save the taxi driver and they had no idea of the whereabouts of his assailants.

While the authorities converged on the scene of their latest crime Lance and Kelbach were strolling into Lolly's Tavern, near Salt Lake City airport. Before anyone had a chance to ask them what they were drinking Lance shot customer James

Sizemore and then ordered the bartender to empty the till. Then both men shot him, before blasting wildly at the customers, two of whom died. But the barman managed to retrieve a weapon from under the counter. He fired at the gunmen as they walked away, but failed to hit either of them.

The duo were captured a couple of hours later and were subsequently convicted on five counts of first degree murder. The mandatory sentence in the state of Utah was death, but an appeal to the United States Supreme Court resulted in the sentences being commuted to life imprisonment because the death penalty was ruled unconstitutional.

The pair remain in prison and are stubbornly unrepentant. 'I haven't any feelings toward the victims,' Walter Kelbach told a reporter from NBC in 1972. 'I don't mind people getting hurt because I just like to watch it.'

BLACK NARCISSUS –

ALTON COLEMAN AND DEBRA BROWN

'IF THERE WAS ANYONE WHO IS EXHIBIT 1 IN AN ARGUMENT FOR THE DEATH PENALTY, IT WAS ALTON COLEMAN.'

JUDGE RICH NIEHAUS

A convicted killer awaiting execution on Death Row once remarked that state executions are nothing more than legalized murders, but the families of the victims might disagree. Those who lost their loved ones to depraved killer couple Alton Coleman and Debra Brown in 1984 might consider their death sentences to be justice duly served.

Predictably, the pair exploited the United States appeals procedure to prolong the inevitable for as long as possible, asking for clemency from the State despite having offered none to their helpless victims. It is not only those who died at their hands who can be called their victims but also those who survived and are now traumatized for life. And then there are the bereaved families who now see the world as a cruel and dangerous place. What

makes their grief even harder to bear is the fact that robber and rapist Alton Coleman was able to stay on the streets, even though the authorities knew he was a menace to society.

As a boy growing up in Waukegan, just north of Chicago, Coleman had been taunted by the local children, who called him 'Pissy' because he frequently wet his trousers. He was the African-American son of a prostitute who entertained her customers while he played in the same room. But his mother sent him to live with his grandmother when he became a burden to her. The experience warped his emotional development and contributed to his desire to dress in women's clothes and find gratification in rough sex. He also exhibited antisocial behaviour and was arrested for vandalism and acts of indecency throughout

Coleman was an insatiable sexual predator who could turn violent if crossed; Brown was borderline mentally retarded

In the end, the forensic evidence linking Coleman and Brown to the attack on the Walters was to prove overwhelming.

his teens. But he presented such a plausible personality in court that he managed to charm the judge and jury time and again.

EVADING JUSTICE

In 1973 he and a friend abducted and raped an elderly woman, but before the case reached the court she was threatened by Coleman and did not press charges, so he was only indicted for robbery. After his two-year stretch he raped another woman but again escaped prosecution for that crime. As before, he was sent down for a

less serious offence. Four years later he was free again and shortly afterwards he was charged with yet another rape. But he evaded a stiff sentence once again. A year later the whole charade was repeated. Each time he was accused of a serious sexual assault or robbery with violence he cited the earlier cases which had not been proven. By this means he raised a reasonable doubt in the mind of the jury, resulting in a nominal sentence for a lesser crime.

What the court did not see was Coleman's sinister side, for he was an insatiable sexual predator who could turn violent if crossed. He routinely threatened witnesses, and forced them to retract their statements on more than one occasion. In 1983 his own sister made a formal complaint against him after he had tried to rape his 14-year-old niece, but shortly afterwards she dropped the charges without explanation. In dismissing the case the judge observed that the mother was clearly 'terrified' of her brother, but without her testimony there was no case to answer.

THE KILLING SPREE BEGINS

A year later, Coleman was accused of the rape and murder of a Chicago girl. She was the daughter of a former friend of his. Coleman must have known that the mother would not be intimidated into keeping silent, so on 2 June 1984 he fled the city with his girlfriend Debra Brown before he could be arrested. Brown had been diagnosed as borderline mentally retarded and a 'dependent personality'. She had been interviewed by the police the day before and would have warned Coleman of the seriousness of the charges hanging over him. He now knew that he was a hunted man and that his luck had run out. With a federal warrant out for his arrest and a witness who would not be cowed, he and Brown hid out for a fortnight before beginning their five-state crime spree. It was to last eight weeks and it involved one of the most intense manhunts ever mounted in America.

Their first victims were two young sisters, Annie and Tamika Turks, who were snatched off the streets of Gary, Indiana in broad daylight. The decomposing body of seven-year-old Tamika was found on 19 June. She had been strangled. Nine-year-old Annie survived a sexual assault, but was severely traumatized after witnessing the vicious murder of her sister. Coleman killed her by jumping on her face and chest until he had punctured her internal organs. It was this and similar acts of brutality that horrified even the most hardened detectives assigned to the case.

A week after Tamika Turks was found, Mr and Mrs Palmer Jones of Dearborn Heights, Michigan were attacked, beaten and robbed in their home. Coleman and Brown were identified as their assailants and as the thieves who had stolen the couple's car. Then on 5 July Coleman and Brown drove into Toledo, Ohio, where they talked their way into the home of Virginia Temple and her children. When they left, Virginia and her eldest daughter, nine-year-old Rachelle, were dead. They

NINE-YEAR-OLD ANNIE SURVIVED A SEXUAL ASSAULT, BUT WAS TRAUMATIZED AFTER WITNESSING COLEMAN KILL HER SISTER BY JUMPING ON HER FACE AND CHEST AND PUNCTURING HER INTERNAL ORGANS

had been strangled. Anxious relatives found the surviving children huddled together and praying that the bad man and his girlfriend would not find their hiding place. Just hours later, Coleman and Brown broke into the home owned by Frank and Dorothy Duvendack, where they bound them with the telephone cable and stole money, valuables and their car.

That afternoon Reverend and Mrs Millard Gay of Dayton, Ohio welcomed two new members to their congregation. Coleman affected his most disarming smile and Brown kept quiet as she played the dutiful girlfriend. While they enjoyed the hospitality of their hosts, the two fugitives listened patiently to an impromptu sermon on the rewards of helping one's neighbours. On 10 July the Gays' good deed even extended to giving the couple a lift to Cincinnati, thus evading the dragnet that had been set up to capture America's most wanted criminals. Then on 11 July an abandoned car belonging to 25-year-old Donna Williams, a resident of Gary, Indiana was found in Detroit. Nearby lay her body. The cause of death was strangulation. Coleman was the last person to have been seen with her.

The couple's next stop was Norwood, Ohio where on 13 July they posed as the potential buyers of a camper van that had been advertised for sale. While discussing the purchase Coleman brained the owner, Harry Walters, with a candlestick and then strangled his wife, Marlene. Mr Walters miraculously survived to identify his wife's killers, who had beaten the poor woman over the head more than twenty times, crushing her skull to fragments. The forensic evidence linking Coleman and Brown to the crime scene was irrefutable.

Two days later, the Walters' car was found in Kentucky. Coleman and Brown had once again swapped vehicles, this time for one owned by Kentucky college professor Oline Carmichael Jnr. The professor was bundled into the boot of his car before being driven back to Dayton, where he was eventually found alive but in a state of shock.

One can only imagine the reaction of Reverend Gay and his wife when their lost sheep turned up at the door brandishing loaded guns and demanding more hospitality, but this time without the sermon. Coleman gave his hosts an assurance.

'I'm not going to kill you, but we generally kills them where we go.'

To the Gays' relief, Coleman and Brown left soon afterwards without resorting to their usual murderous violence. But they took Millard Gay's car and doubled back towards Evanston, exchanging it for another one en route, after killing the elderly driver.

COLEMAN GAVE HIS HOSTS AN ASSURANCE. 'I'M NOT GOING TO KILL YOU, BUT WE GENERALLY KILLS THEM WHERE WE GO'

THE END OF THE LINE

On 20 July 1984 the couple's merciless murderous spree ended quietly in their home town of Waukegan, Illinois without a shot being fired. A former neighbour recognized Coleman as he and Brown crossed the street and he telephoned the police. The couple were surrounded as they sat in a local park and they were taken into custody still protesting their innocence.

The police were presented with an open and shut case. No confessions were needed. The forensic evidence was compelling and there were a number of surviving eyewitnesses. Coleman would not be able to threaten them all. The only problem facing the authorities was deciding where to hold the trial, because the crimes had taken place in six states. In the end 50 law enforcement officers from the affected states held a strategy meeting, at which Ohio was chosen. United States attorney Dan Webb explained their decision to the press.

'We are convinced that prosecution (in Ohio) can most quickly and most likely result in the swiftest imposition of the death penalty against Alton Coleman and Debra Brown.'

To the dismay of his surviving victims Alton Coleman was able to stave off his execution for 16 years by invoking every constitutional loophole that his legal team could exploit. He claimed to have been represented by 'ineffective counsel', that the jurors at his trial were racially biased and that he suffered from an abusive childhood and a personality disorder. When these arguments failed he instructed his lawyers to protest that his rights would be violated by having his execution broadcast over closed-circuit television. But he was only delaying the inevitable. On the morning of

Lethal injections feature potassium chloride (stops heart) sodium thiopental (barbiturate) and pancuronium (relaxant)

26 April 2002 46-year-old Coleman was strapped to a gurney in the death chamber at the Southern Ohio Correctional Facility near Lucasville and given a lethal injection consisting of three different chemicals, which sent him into oblivion. Among those who witnessed his exit was Harry Walters, whose wife Marlene had been beaten to death.

Brown had her death sentence commuted to life imprisonment on account of her low intelligence level and her master-slave relationship with the domineering Coleman. But she remained unrepentant. During her trial she sent the judge a note. 'I killed the bitch and I don't give a damn. I had fun out of it.'

SHE MADE ME DO IT –

ALVIN AND JUDITH NEELEY

Gravedigger John Hancock of Georgia considers himself one of the luckiest men alive.

On 3 October 1982 he and his fiancée, Janice Kay Chatman, accepted a lift from a young woman who shot him in the back and left him for dead and then sped off with his terrified companion.

After his recovery, Hancock learnt that he and Janice were the latest victims of a pitiless pair of serial killers who were suspects in a murder inquiry. The assassins were also sought for questioning in respect of two separate incidents – in the first one, shots had been fired at a victim's house and on the second occasion, another home in the same area had been firebombed. Hancock's miraculous escape proved to be the turning point for a case that had been confounding the Georgia police for a month.

While he was giving his statement at police headquarters, Hancock quite by chance overheard a recording of a threatening telephone call made by a young woman to the family who had been firebombed. He immediately identified the voice as that of the girl who had shot him and abducted Janice Chatman.

At first detectives were sceptical. It seemed incredible that Hancock and Chatman would accept a ride from a stranger simply because she said she was lonely and would appreciate their company. Their initial thoughts were that Hancock had invented the story to divert suspicion from his part in the disappearance of his fiancée and that

> BY CHANCE HANCOCK OVERHEARD A THREATENING PHONE CALL MADE TO A FAMILY WHO HAD BEEN FIREBOMBED. HE IMMEDIATELY IDENTIFIED THE VOICE

Alvin and Judith Neeley were a lawless trailer trash couple with a record as long as the Mississippi

The Neeleys were constantly on the move, robbing convenience stores and gas stations to finance their wayward lifestyle

he had sustained the bullet wound in a struggle. But his insistence that he had been shot by the woman who had made the recording – and the fact that his description of her car matched a description given by a witness in the firebombing incident – convinced police to take his evidence seriously. Furthermore, Hancock claimed that the woman had two young children in the back of the car, which had convinced Janice and him that she was genuine.

THE 'NIGHTRIDER'

Hancock's story also contained further clues to the woman's identity and that of her unseen male accomplice. During the drive the woman had talked to a man over her CB (Citizens' Band) radio. She had called him the 'Nightrider'. John was a CB radio user himself and he noticed that the frequency she was using was too weak to reach someone she claimed was transmitting from the next state. He then became anxious when they drove out of town and a large intimidating figure approached the car. The man introduced himself as the Nightrider and told them to follow him to a spot where they could get some of the finest hooch in Georgia. By the time the two cars came to a halt Hancock had no idea where they were.

When he got out to relieve himself he realized that the young woman had followed him into the forest and was holding a gun to his head. She ordered him to walk off the path into the trees and then she fired, hitting him in the right shoulder. But she did not check that he was dead. When he heard the cars driving away he staggered down to the highway and flagged down a passing trucker who took him to hospital.

The bullet recovered from his shoulder was analyzed by ballistics and the descriptions of the two cars – a brown Dodge with white stripes and a red Granada – were noted in the case file, together with an artist's sketch of the duo, drawn to match John's description. It was at this stage in the investigation that the abduction of Janice Chatman, the ongoing murder inquiry and the two residential attacks converged.

FINDING A LINK

Detective Sergeant Kenneth Kines re-interviewed Linda Adair and Kenneth Dooley, the homeowners who had been subjected to the threatening phone calls, the arson attack and the shooting. They had both worked at the Youth Development Centre for troubled girls, so he asked them if any incident might have given one of the female inmates grounds to hold a grudge. They denied any suggestion of institutional abuse and repeated that they had nothing in common other than the fact that they had both worked at the YDC. They lived separate lives and could not think of any girl who might be targeting them.

But Detective Kines was convinced that there was a link. He trawled through the files at the YDC searching for a troubled teen who might fit the profile and before long he had narrowed the list down to five names. Among them was that of Judith Ann Neeley, whose physical description

happened to match that given by Hancock and the other witnesses. Her file also contained the fact that she had been arrested for armed robbery and was familiar with firearms. When Linda Adair, the YDC worker whose home had been firebombed, heard that Janice Chatman's abductor had two children in tow she remembered that a young offender at the centre would have had two children of the same age. Her name was Judith Neeley. Adair had kept photographs of her and her husband Alvin, which she now passed to the police. When these were shown to John Hancock he identified

When Hancock went to relieve himself in the forest, he found the young woman had followed him.

Neeley as his attacker and her husband Alvin as the elusive Nightrider. The couple were being held in Tennessee on other charges, so it was simply a matter of asking the neighbouring state to have the suspects transported to Georgia, where they would take part in an identity parade.

Alvin and Judith were a lawless trailer trash couple with a record as long as the Mississippi, including hold-ups and car thefts from Georgia to the Mexican border. Judith's husband was 12 years her senior, a flabby hog of a man who was described by Detective Kines as 'a pathetic character if ever there was one'. Yet the 18-year-old Judith was devoted to him. In 1980 the pair were convicted of robbery and passing stolen cheques. Alvin went to prison for five years and Judith was detained at the YDC, where she gave birth to twins. While there, she alleged staff had sexually abused her. Perhaps she wanted attention. The police investigated but found no evidence to substantiate her claims, which only served to fuel her resentment.

THE CHILDREN WERE A LURE

Shortly after Judith's release in 1981 she was caught robbing a grocery store, but she wriggled out of a prison sentence on account of the twins. When Alvin was released six months later they had to take the children along with them wherever they went. So the children were in the back of the car when they sprayed YDC worker Kenneth Dooley's home with gunfire and threw a Molotov cocktail at Linda Adair's house.

The children were also used to lure 13-year-old Lisa Ann Millican into the car at the Riverbend Mall in Rome, Georgia, coincidentally the site of a robbery Judith had carried out two years earlier. While police searched for the girl in vain, they received three anonymous phone calls from a female who directed them to the site where the body could be found, but no corpse was recovered. More calls followed. This time there was a more detailed description of the location and a female officer at the YDC was accused of complicity in the crime. Clearly someone was out to implicate the centre, even to the extent of murdering an innocent young girl in order to cast suspicion on the staff. Whatever the caller's motive might have been, the police took the tip seriously and decided to search the area again more thoroughly.

At nightfall on 29 September 1982 a search

ALVIN AND JUDITH HAD KEPT LISA CHAINED TO A BED IN A HOTEL ROOM, WHILE ALVIN RAPED HER IN THE PRESENCE OF HIS CHILDREN

team spotted a girl's body at the bottom of a canyon. There was a single bullet in her back. She had evidently been murdered and had then been thrown 80 feet to the rocks below. A pair of bloody jeans was found nearby, which did not belong to the victim, and three empty syringes were recovered from the scene. Back at the crime laboratory these syringes were found to contain traces of drain cleaner. It had been injected into the girl's neck, causing the fat under her skin to boil. The pain must have been excruciating. The victim, now identified as Lisa Ann Millican, had also been sexually assaulted. It later transpired that Alvin and Judith had kept Lisa chained to a bed in a hotel room, while Alvin raped her in the presence of their children. It was apparently his idea to kill her by injecting her with drain cleaner, but it was Judith who carried out the gruesome execution.

Six times she jabbed the needle into the screaming teen, until she realized that it was not going to prove fatal. It was then that she shot Lisa and pushed her over the edge on to the rocks below.

Within a week Judith was looking for a second victim. She failed to persuade a woman waiting at a payphone to accept a lift, mainly because the woman had just called her husband so that he could pick her up.

But the intended victim had also felt that there was something disturbing about Judith, which made her uneasy about accepting a ride.

It was shortly after this incident that Judith picked up John Hancock and Janice Chatman. When she had disposed of John, Judith rejoined Alvin and they drove Janice to a motel where they raped her repeatedly, then shot her and dumped the body in a creek. But before the couple could slaughter more innocents they were arrested for passing forged money orders in nearby Murfreesboro, where they were questioned by detectives who knew exactly who they were dealing with.

There was no let-up in the interrogation that turned the screws on the flustered Alvin. Finally he confessed to 15 murders, all of which he claimed had been instigated by his wife. She was a control freak, he said, and he feared that she would kill him if he double-crossed her. He laid all the crimes on her and she initially took the blame – or the credit as she would see it. But he was not entirely unco-operative. He drew detectives a map indicating the location of Janice Chatman's body, so he could not deny his part in disposing of the corpse.

THE BRIDE OF FRANKENSTEIN SYNDROME

The evidence against Alvin was largely circumstantial in the case of Lisa Millican but it was strong enough to secure a conviction for the abduction, rape and murder of Janice Chatman. So the Tennessee district attorney decided to underwrite the risk by splitting the couple. He ordered the prosecutors in his own state to prepare the case against Alvin for the kidnap and murder of Janice Chatman, which would mean a statutory life sentence, but he extradited Judith to Alabama to be tried for the first degree murder of Lisa Millican, which carried the death penalty. She also faced two other counts of abduction with intent to terrorize and abduction with intent to harm.

An insanity plea was thrown out after Judith was deemed fit to plead by the Alabama state

Judith held a gun to Hancock's head and ordered him to walk off the path into the trees, then she fired

psychiatrist, so her attorney, Robert French Jnr., fell back on the 'battered woman' defence. On the opening day of the trial at the DeKalb County Courthouse at Fort Payne in March 1983, French portrayed his client as a puppet controlled by her violent and abusive husband, who was not present to defend himself. In the ensuing days French called Alvin's first wife to the stand to testify to her husband's violent outbursts and the physical scars that she still bore.

Then Judith was sworn in. She described how she had committed the crimes under duress and at her husband's direction. Alvin had ordered her to kidnap girls for him to rape and she did not possess the will to resist. She had given Lisa the fatal injections of drain cleaner out of compassion, to end her suffering, but she had no idea that it would take so many to kill her.

The only anecdotal evidence to support her assertion came from John Hancock, who told the court that he had heard Alvin twice order her to hurry before she shot him. But the district attorney countered that Alvin had not ordered her to take him out and kill him. John Hancock had left the car to urinate and Judith had followed him into the forest on her own initiative. She then shot him when she could have let him escape if she had wanted to. The district attorney also succeeded in entering into evidence the letters that Judith had written to Alvin after their arrest.

These contradicted the version of events that she was giving on the stand and under oath. Clearly she was a woman who would perjure herself and sacrifice her partner to save her own skin.

French made a last ditch plea for leniency by citing a psychiatric condition known as 'coercive persuasion', in which sufferers instinctively do what they are told because they have been conditioned to do so after being subjected to brutality and isolation. But the State's expert witness, psychiatrist Alexander Salillas, refuted the idea by saying that even battered women still had a choice. According to the examination which he had carried out, he said, Judith Neeley knew the difference between right and wrong and had made a conscious decision to commit murder.

When the jury retired on 21 March 1983 they spent the evening in deliberation and then returned a verdict the next morning. It was 'guilty on all counts'. It is thought that the jury recommended that Judith be sentenced to life imprisonment rather than death on account of her age, but the judge ruled that her actions betrayed a callous nature fully justifying the death penalty. Her crimes had been uncommonly cruel

and many who attended the trial or who had been privy to her interrogations concurred that she had been the instigator and Alvin had been the duplicitous servant.

In March 1987 the United States Supreme Court rejected her appeal and two years later it upheld the death sentence. But before it could be carried out it was commuted to life imprisonment without parole by the then governor of Alabama, Fob James, who justified his highly controversial decision by saying that the jury had recommended that she serve life and that he felt duty-bound to honour their recommendation.

Neeley's tender years persuaded some to lobby for the reinstatement of her right to parole and in July 2002 Montgomery Circuit Court judge Gene Reese ruled that she could be considered for release but not until January 2014. However, even if she was granted parole in Alabama, the Tennessee district attorney's decision to try Judith and Alvin separately means that she could still stand trial in Georgia for the rape and murder of Janice Chatman.

The law may have its flaws, but it seems that it will not be mocked in the southern states.

WHEN SHE HAD DISPOSED OF JOHN, JUDITH REJOINED ALVIN AND THEY DROVE JANICE TO A MOTEL WHERE THEY RAPED HER REPEATEDLY, THEN SHOT HER

CHAPTER 4

PLEASURE AND PAIN

Many theories have been offered as to how and why normal sexual impulses and desires turn into sadistic fantasies. None has proven completely satisfactory. Not all victims of abuse become abusers; not all control freaks become rapists; not all chronic fantasists are driven to act out their fantasies. Sadistic sex killers and serial rapists are often branded as 'insane', but the chilling fact remains that these individuals still retain enough self-control to ensure they evade detection for as long as possible.

SUFFER LITTLE CHILDREN –
THE MOORS MURDERERS, IAN BRADY AND MYRA HINDLEY

One month after the arrest of the Moors Murderers, Ian Brady and Myra Hindley, Britain repealed the death penalty. But when the sickening details of the crimes perpetrated by the two sadistic child killers became public knowledge, many in the country believed the authorities might have been too hasty. A state-sponsored execution would not have been murder, they argued, but a mercy killing.

Long after Hindley's death in prison in 2002 the sullen, defiant faces of the killers continued to haunt the nation. Behind their grim thin lips and dead eyes they looked smugly satisfied that they had escaped the ultimate penalty and had been kept in comparative comfort at society's expense. They had also been protected from the wrath of an outraged media, whose impotent anger must have fed Brady's warped ego. An enlightened society had given them life in the belief that incarceration and isolation might force them to confront their personal demons and wrestle with their consciences. If the judiciary had subscribed to that theory they were to be sorely disappointed.

Brady and Hindley showed no remorse and they stubbornly refused to comply with repeated requests to lead police to the burial places of two of their young victims. The deviant duo had no consciences to prick. They were incapable of feeling empathy or compassion and they had shown their victims no mercy. Nor did they have any feelings of regret, other than for the fact that they had been caught. The psychologists and psychiatrists who evaluated their mental state described them as disturbed, delusional, obsessive and unbalanced, but in the words of the tabloids they were simply 'evil'.

Inside Broadmoor, Britain's formidable fortress for the criminally insane, Brady could strike up friendships with the likes of Peter

> THE DEVIANT DUO HAD NO CONSCIENCES TO PRICK. THEY WERE INCAPABLE OF FEELING EMPATHY OR COMPASSION

Brady was the illegitimate son of a waitress; Hindley was attracted by his sullen manner and introspective nature

Fatal attraction: Brady and Hindley met in a chemical factory in Manchester where they both worked

Sutcliffe, the 'Yorkshire Ripper', and poisoner Graham Young, with whom he played chess on an almost daily basis. He even carried on a lengthy correspondence with the United States serial killer John Wayne Gacy. If he could not be on the outside gratifying his craving for inflicting pain on others, he would experience it vicariously through letters exchanged with his blood brothers. Like so many serial killers before and after him, notoriety was the culmination of his criminal career and the fulfilment of his fantasy. It compensated him for his failure to achieve anything of real or lasting value. In crude terms, he convinced himself that if his disadvantaged background prevented him from becoming a hero, he would devote himself to becoming a villain. Better negative recognition than none at all.

A NEED FOR DOMINANCE

Brady was born Ian Duncan Stewart on 2 January 1938. The illegitimate son of a waitress, he never learned the identity of his father. He spent a troubled childhood in foster care and, although he was intelligent, he was also lazy, defiant and violent, which brought him into conflict with his foster parents, his teachers and ultimately the police. From an early age he exhibited the classic symptoms of an emergent psychosis – he enjoyed torturing animals and had a morbid fascination with books on every aspect of sadism.

But neither his foster parents nor the school confronted him about his disturbing behaviour. In his teens he took to quoting passages from Hitler's *Mein Kampf* and in an effort to attract attention and assert himself he openly admitted to an admiration for the Nazis.

Myra Hindley found Brady fascinating. They met in 1961 at the Manchester chemical factory where they were both employed. She was just 19 years old, dull and emotionally insecure. Her father's violent alcoholic rages had forced her from the family home and at the age of 15 she had witnessed the death of a friend by drowning, an accident for which she felt personally responsible. Still a virgin, she was attracted by Brady's sullen manner and his introspective nature. The longer he ignored her, the more intense her infatuation for him became. When he finally condescended to sleep with her she felt privileged and he in turn was empowered by her admiration.

In the following weeks she would do anything he asked, be it sadomasochistic sex or armed robbery. But although the couple planned a series of bank robberies, it was not money that got Brady's adrenalin pumping – it was dominance, power and pain. Only by repeatedly exerting his authority over others could Brady strengthen his ideal self-image, that of a man who was feared and obeyed. In his more lucid moments he knew that no one would fear him unless he threatened them with violence and even then an adult might easily overpower him. The only people he could intimidate were children, so children it would have to be.

A CHILLING EPISODE

On 12 July 1963 Myra borrowed a van and drove through the streets of Manchester while Brady rode behind on a motorcycle. When he saw a likely target he signalled to her by flashing his headlight. She would then pull over and offer the youngster a lift. Their first victim was teenager Pauline Reade. She was abducted and taken to the moors, where she was raped and beaten about the head with a shovel before having her throat cut. The next victim was even younger – 12-year-old John Kilbride was abducted on 23 November. He was stabbed and strangled and then sexually molested after death by Brady, who buried him out on the moors.

The next summer the pair bought a van of their own in which they kidnapped 12-year-old Keith Bennett on 16 June. Again Brady strangled and molested him, but this time Myra took photographs to prolong their pleasure.

FROM AN EARLY AGE, BRADY ENJOYED TORTURING ANIMALS AND HAD A MORBID FASCINATION WITH BOOKS ON EVERY ASPECT OF SADISM. HE TOOK TO QUOTING FROM *MEIN KAMPF*

It was like a scene from Grimm's Fairy Tales when the couple lured 10-year-old Lesley Ann Downey from a Christmas fair on 24 December 1964 with the promise of sweets and toys. This time the victim was raped and strangled in their home while Myra recorded the child's screams and her pitiful pleas for her mother.

When the tape was subsequently played in court, it was described by the newspapers as one of the most chilling and distressing episodes in British criminal history.

But Ian Brady was not finished. On 5 October 1965 he abducted teenager Edward Evans and then invited his 17-year-old brother-in-law David home to watch the fun. David was a petty thief and a known admirer of Ian. The pair had planned a series of robberies which they did not have the courage to carry out, but Brady still thought that he could rely on David to do what he was told. But David was all talk.

When he saw Brady pick up an axe and hack Evans to death he made his excuses and left.

'It was a horrible scene. The lad was screaming and trying to get away. Ian just kept hitting him terrible blows on the head, neck and shoulders... I was frightened to death, my stomach was churning. There was blood everywhere, on the walls, the fireplace, all over.'

PICNICKING BY THE GRAVES

David Smith ran home and telephoned the police. When they arrived, the body of Edward Evans was still in the house. It was wrapped in a plastic sheet in the upstairs bedroom and the murder weapon was nearby. From the detectives' point of view they had been handed a sure-fire prosecution on a plate, but there was more.

A search of the house revealed a notebook with a list of names, including several missing persons, and there were photographs of Hindley and Brady posing and picnicking at various places on the moors.

It was later discovered that these were the locations of the graves of some of their victims. The police found a left-luggage ticket among Myra's belongings that she had been using as a bookmark. When the suitcase was collected from Manchester railway station it was found to contain pornographic material, various weapons, ammunition, graphic photographs of the torture

Without mercy: Hindley recorded Lesley Ann Downey's screams and her pitiful pleas for her mother

Banged up: Brady and Hindley leave Chester Crown Court, heading for long-term incarceration

inflicted on Lesley Ann Downey and a reel of audio tape recording the child's torment and murder.

In a pathetic attempt to save their own skins by deflecting the blame on to someone else, Brady and Hindley accused David Smith of being the instigator of their crimes. But their fingerprints were on the contents of the suitcase and the axe handle and it was their handwriting in the notebook.

The jury took just four hours to return a guilty verdict on three charges of murder for Brady and two for Hindley. With the death penalty no longer an option the judge could only sentence them to life imprisonment on each count.

In a last spiteful act neither of them would identify the grave sites of Pauline Reade or Keith Bennett, but despite their refusal the remains of Pauline Reade were recovered in July 1987, after it was noticed that there were disturbances to the soil and the vegetation in one particular spot on the Pennine moors. But Keith Bennett's grave remains unknown to this day, despite repeated pleas by the police and his mother.

Dangerous dogs are routinely put down, but in 'civilized' countries we advocate that predatory murderers and sadistic serial killers should be imprisoned indefinitely, or at least be confined to a mental institution. The hope is that they can be rehabilitated, even if they cannot be released.

Some might say that society is too merciful.

MUMMY AND DADDY DEAREST –

FRED AND ROSE WEST

The public is understandably keen to distance itself from serial killers, so it demonizes them by referring to them as 'monsters'. But in the case of Rosemary and Fred West those words get right to the dark heart of the depraved couple's psychosis.

Rosemary's mother was pregnant with her daughter when she was forced to undergo electroshock therapy for depression in 1953. One can only imagine what those violent surges of electricity must have done to her baby, who was born in November of that same year. All the indications are that Rosemary Letts was emotionally and mentally retarded. As a child she would rock her head backwards and forwards for hours until she was in a trance-like state,

a habit that earned her the nickname 'Dozy Rosie'. Any resulting damage to her brain or her emotional development would certainly have been compounded by a brutal upbringing at the hands of her schizophrenic father, who punished the children severely for every real and imagined infraction of his rigid rules.

Her brother Andrew is still smarting from the emotional scars.

'If he felt we were in bed too late, he would throw a bucket of cold water over us. He would order us to dig the garden, and that meant the whole garden. Then he would inspect it like an army officer, and if he was not satisfied, we would have to do it all over again. We were not allowed to speak and play like normal children. If we were noisy, he would go for

AS A CHILD, ROSE WOULD ROCK HER HEAD BACK AND FORWARDS FOR HOURS UNTIL SHE WAS IN A TRANCE-LIKE STATE, WHICH EARNED HER THE NICKNAME 'DOZY ROSIE'

East West Home's Best: Fred and Rose West do their best impression of an ordinary happy couple...

Family Guy: Fred West at a wedding surrounded by well-scrubbed children

us with a belt or chunk of wood. He would beat you black and blue until mum got in between us. Then she would get a good hiding.'

Things were made worse by the fact that Rose's father's unskilled work was poorly paid, which led to continuous violent arguments.

INSATIABLE APPETITE

Fred was born into a family of farm labourers in the Herefordshire village of Much Marcle in 1941. He was one of six children and he was his mother's favourite. When Fred was caned at school, which was often, she marched in and told the headmaster off, which gave the other boys more reason to laugh at him. She indulged him and she defended his antisocial behaviour, which included hanging out with the roughest kids, shoplifting and having sex with underage girls, the younger the better. But when at the age of 20 he was accused of forcing himself on a 13-year-old, even his own dysfunctional family disowned him.

He only escaped a jail sentence because medical reports supported his claim to be suffering from epileptic fits.

There can be little doubt that Fred was brain-damaged following a motorbike accident which put him in a coma when he was 17 years old.

When he finally left hospital with a metal plate screwed inside his skull, he suffered a second serious fall when a girl pushed him off a fire escape. People who knew him at the time agreed that after these incidents he became more aggressive – but he had not been a balanced or pleasant person to begin with. The girl who pushed him off the fire escape had done so because he had put his hand up her skirt. He had a reputation as a sexually aggressive youth and he was known as a compulsive liar.

For instance, he told girls that he had made one of his sisters pregnant and that his father had sexually abused his own daughters. Presumably he was out to shock them and make a name for himself as a notorious character in the village.

His appetite for sex was insatiable. He took a job driving an ice cream van so he could meet young girls and at around that time he married a prostitute, Catherine Bernadette (Rena) Costello, whom he had known since his teens. She was then pregnant with Charmaine, a child fathered by an Asian lover, so when Fred sought reconciliation with his family in 1962 he concocted a convoluted story that he and Rena had adopted a child of mixed-race parents.

But even the former prostitute found her husband's insatiable sexual appetite unusual.

He demanded oral sex, bondage and sodomy at all hours of the day and night. Straight sex did not interest him at all. Nevertheless she bore him a daughter, Anna Marie. After an accident in which he killed a young boy with his ice cream van, he and Rena moved to Gloucester, where he took a job in a slaughterhouse. Surrounded by cadavers he became morbidly obsessed with blood, dismemberment and necrophilia.

It was all too much for Rena. She and Fred separated, leaving him to take up with a mutual friend of theirs, Anna McFall. By her own admission Rena was incapable of caring for the children so she entrusted them to Anna and Fred, although she later told detectives that he was a sexual pervert and unfit to be a father.

She was right. In early 1967 Fred murdered Anna when she became pregnant. She had wanted him to divorce Rena and marry her. He dismembered her body and disposed of it near the trailer park where they lived. Then Rena returned and supported them by going back on the streets. Fred made no secret of his desire to have sex with Charmaine and Rena's drug-taking made her too disconnected from reality to raise any objection.

FRED DEMANDED ORAL SEX, BONDAGE AND SODOMY AT ALL HOURS OF THE DAY AND NIGHT. STRAIGHT SEX DID NOT INTEREST HIM AT ALL

But that was not Fred's only crime. It is believed that in the years before he met Rosemary Letts he had already abducted and murdered a dozen or more girls in the Gloucester area, crimes for which there is significant but circumstantial evidence. However, there has been no confession from the prime suspect.

THE MONSTERS MEET

Rose suspected none of this when they met on 29 November 1968. Fred was doing his delivery round for a local baker and he just saw the bespectacled, overweight 15-year-old as another potential conquest. She was more than willing. Having no innate sense of what constituted inappropriate behaviour, Rose thought nothing of fondling her own brother or making herself available to any man in the village who showed an interest. It is said that she was raped by a local man and had an incestuous relationship with her father to avoid the beatings, though this might have been malicious local gossip. But she was certainly promiscuous.

Once they became intimate Fred realized that he had found a playmate who would do anything to please him, for Rose was incapable of finding any sexual act degrading. Her only problem, as he saw it, was her volatile temper. In 1969 Fred was imprisoned for theft and 16-year-old Rose moved into their new house in Midland Road. She was going to take care of Charmaine and Anna Marie and prepare for the birth of her own child, Heather, who she was carrying at the time. But Rose was not made to be a mother because she continually lost her temper with the children. Then one day in the summer of 1971 she lost control completely. She explained Charmaine's absence to Anna Marie by telling her that Rena had returned to collect her, but in all likelihood she had murdered her. The child's body was found under the kitchen floor 24 years later, with the fingers, toes and kneecaps removed, a signature of Fred's. When Rena turned up later looking for her daughter Fred dispatched her too. Again he mutilated the corpse by cutting off the fingers and the toes.

That was not the only fetish he indulged in during their early life together. Fred liked to invite strangers back to the house to have sex with Rose, while he watched through a peephole. If they paid, it was a bonus. But all he really wanted was to watch. And the more bizarre and sadistic

THE CHILD'S BODY WAS FOUND UNDER THE KITCHEN FLOOR 24 YEARS LATER, WITH THE FINGERS, TOES AND KNEECAPS REMOVED, A SIGNATURE OF FRED'S

the act, the more he enjoyed it. Despite their unconventional relationship Fred and Rose still felt the need to get married, which they did in January 1972. Six months later their daughter Mae West was born.

The house in Midland Road was now too small for the family so a move was in order. That summer they moved into an address that was to become synonymous with horror – 25 Cromwell Street. Fred told a neighbour that he thought the cellar would make the perfect torture chamber. She naturally assumed he was joking.

THE MOVE TO 25 CROMWELL STREET

Once the room had been soundproofed Fred and Rosemary took their eight-year-old daughter Anna Marie there. She was bound and gagged and told that she should consider herself fortunate that her parents cared enough to make sure she would know how to satisfy her husband. Then her father raped her. Afterwards they threatened to beat her if she told anyone. She was kept off school for days afterwards because of her injuries. It was not the last time she was abused in this way. Fred saw his children as his to use and abuse.

It could all have ended there because the Wests soon found themselves in court accused of raping 17-year-old Caroline Owens, their live-in nanny. But despite Fred's long record of sexual offences the magistrate believed his version of events. He accepted Fred's assurance that Caroline had consented and the couple were let off with a fine. It was a fatal mistake.

The next nanny, Lynda Gough, was murdered, dismembered and buried under the floor of the garage. Her fingers, toes and kneecaps had been removed, as was usual with Fred's victims.

And all the time the Wests continued to act, in public at least, like a normal working-class family. Another son, Stephen, was born in August 1973 and a few months later another corpse was buried under the foundations of a new extension. No one commented or complained that these 'home improvements' were being carried out long after midnight.

Many more girls entered 25 Cromwell Street and did not leave alive. Fifteen-year-old Carol Ann Cooper was killed in November 1973 and in the following month university student Lucy Partington was tortured for a week and then killed. She was followed by 21-year-old Therese Siegenthaler, 15-year-old Shirley Hubbard and 18-year-old Juanita Mott. Each of them had been treated like captive animals and had then suffered unspeakably cruel deaths.

In 1977 refurbishments were carried out on the upper floors to accommodate a number of lodgers, including 18-year-old prostitute Shirley Robinson. Bisexual Shirley soon became sexually active with both Fred and Rose and was made pregnant by Fred at about the same time that Rose learned that she was herself pregnant by another man. Rose gave birth to a daughter named Tara in December of that year while Shirley and her unborn child were murdered by Fred, who had been given an ultimatum by his jealous wife. Mother and baby were buried in the back garden. A year later, in 1978, the Wests brought another child, Louise, into their nightmare world.

Meanwhile, the garden cemetery was groaning with bodies, the latest being teenage runaway Alison Chambers, who was raped and tortured in

'Home improvements' were not about keeping up with the Joneses: nanny Lynda Gough was buried under the floor of the garage

1979. In spite of all of this, the Wests kept having more children. In June 1980 their seventh child, Barry, entered the world and two years later, in April 1982, another girl, also called Rosemary, was born. This time Fred was not the father. In July 1983 yet another infant, Lucyanna, was added to the overcrowded house at Cromwell Street.

THE ENEMY WITHIN

But time was running out for the Wests. The one factor they had not considered was the fact that their enemy was not without but within. They could hide their activities from the neighbours and the authorities when their children were young and dependent on them, but soon their offspring would be old enough to realize that their abuse did not have to be suffered in silence. They would be the ones to expose their perverted parents.

Heather was the first one to confide in a friend, but she was murdered and disposed of before the allegations could be investigated. Her parents quashed all enquiries by claiming that she had run away with a boyfriend and that they had no idea of her whereabouts. They claimed that she was a lesbian who was aggressive, a drug addict and impossible to control. There was no point in looking for her, because she could be anywhere. Perhaps she was making a living as a prostitute. It was a cruel and malicious lie.

But the horror had to come to an end some time.

And in August 1992 a young girl who had survived torture and rape at the hands of Fred and Rose West blurted out her story to a friend, who went straight to the police and reported what she had been told. She spoke to Detective Constable Hazel Savage, who had already come across similar allegations against Fred. Not only that, she had actually interviewed Rena Costello 15 years earlier. She finally had sufficient grounds to request a search warrant, but it only gave the police the power to search for pornography and evidence of child abuse. With so many young children in the house the police had to tread very carefully so as not to endanger them further. If they rushed into making an arrest and the suspects were freed on a technicality the children could be placed in jeopardy.

On 6 August a thorough search was made of the house and sufficient material was recovered to support the prosecution of both parents. Fred was charged with the rape and sodomy of a minor and Rose was charged with being an accessory. But these charges were a holding action in order to separate the predators from their prey. As the investigation got under way the stories of abuse became ever more horrific, which convinced the police that they were getting closer to a conviction. But there was still no incontrovertible proof that baby Charmaine, her mother Rena and the West's daughter Heather had been murdered, and no one had even considered the possibility that the Wests had claimed other victims. Yet as often happens in such cases it was dogged routine detective work that finally led to the unpalatable truth.

Detective Constable Savage knew she did not yet have sufficient grounds to request a warrant for the excavation of 25 Cromwell Street, but her request would be taken seriously if she exhausted all avenues of inquiry into the whereabouts of Heather West. The Wests insisted she was still alive, but DC Savage had been unable to trace her movements through her employment records, the Tax Office or the National Health Service. There was no record of Heather in the system. She had ceased to exist.

And then the unthinkable happened. The case collapsed just when it appeared to be airtight. Two crucial witnesses withdrew their co-operation for reasons which were never disclosed and the police had no choice but to release Fred. His wife

THE GARDEN CEMETERY WAS GROANING WITH BODIES, THE LATEST BEING ALISON CHAMBERS. IN SPITE OF ALL THIS, THE WESTS KEPT HAVING MORE CHILDREN

was already at home, passing the days watching videos and eating chocolates. Now the need for forensic evidence was critical. Fortunately DC Savage was supported by her superior, Detective Superintendent John Bennett, who shared her suspicions. They decided that they would not find what they were looking for if they did not commit all their available resources to uncovering the truth. And if Fred and Rosemary refused to admit their guilt, they would have to unearth the proof, literally.

DIGGING UP THE EVIDENCE

Fred was out on 24 February 1994 when the police knocked on the front door of 25 Cromwell Street and presented Rose with a search warrant. They were going to dig up the garden and demolish the extension in a hunt for Heather's remains. They were still clearing the ground the following morning when Fred suddenly confessed to killing his daughter. Then he recanted.

'Heather's alive and well,' he told the bemused detectives. 'She's possibly at the moment in Bahrain working for a drug cartel. She had a Mercedes, a chauffeur and a new birth certificate.'

But he repeated his confession when he heard that human bones had been found in the garden, even though the police had not said that they had been identified as Heather's remains. They had an argument, he said. He had seized her by the throat in the struggle and she had stopped breathing. It was an accident. But then he had to dispose of the body because no one would have believed him, so he dismembered her in the bath. But first he had made sure she was really dead by garrotting her with a pair of tights.

'I didn't want to touch her while she was alive. If I'd have started cutting her leg or her throat and she'd have suddenly come alive...'

Then he cut off her head and limbs and dumped the dismembered body in the dustbin. When it was dark he retrieved the sacks and buried them in the garden. The police confronted Rosemary with the news of his confession but she denied any knowledge of it, claiming that she was away at the time.

Three sets of remains were discovered in the garden and there were nine more in the cellar. There were so many that Fred could not remember who had been buried where. The police suggested that he had been responsible for many more murders, and a dozen or more unreported rapes, in and around Gloucester since the early 1970s, but again he could not remember details of names or places. There were too many.

As the interrogations continued Rose gave a poor performance as the deceived and innocent wife. No one was fooled.

On 13 December 1994, Frederick West was charged with twelve murders, but he did not live long enough to face justice. On 1 January 1995 he hanged himself in his cell using strips of bed sheets.

Rose was left to face her accusers alone on 3 October 1995. Her own daughter Anna Marie made a credible witness, but Rose condemned herself by her arrogant performance in the witness box. Her angry outbursts left no doubt in the jurors' minds that she was an active participant in the abuse of her own children. Fred's taped confession was played in court but although he was heard to say again and again that his wife was innocent,

Three bodies were discovered in the garden; Fred had killed so many people he couldn't remember who was buried where

he had been revealed as a compulsive liar on so many counts that his words had the opposite effect. And then there was the evidence of Janet Leach, an impartial civilian witness to Fred's police interviews. She told the court that Fred had told her that he had agreed to take the blame even though Rosemary had been guilty of the murders of Charmaine and Shirley Robinson.

There was no doubting the outcome when the jury finally retired to consider their verdict. Rosemary West was guilty on all ten counts of murder with a life sentence for each life so cruelly cut short. The house at 25 Cromwell Street was demolished on the orders of Gloucester Council, but the knowledge of what went on there lingers to this day.

Sadly, one can only imagine what horrific memories remain in the minds of the children of Fred and Rosemary West and the surviving victims and their families.

DEATH FACTORY –

LEONARD LAKE AND CHARLES NG

The most serious murder cases are often solved because of a simple stroke of luck, the merest coincidence, or a momentary slip by the cautious killer, which leads investigators to uncover the remains of victims they perhaps did not even know were missing.

Who knows how many more innocent people might have fallen victim to sexual sadists Leonard Lake and Charles Chitat Ng if they had resisted the compulsion to steal a $20 vice from a South City DIY store on 2 June 1985? But even as police closed in on their custom-built torture chamber in the forested hills above San Francisco, it was already too late for an estimated 25 victims.

Lake and Ng's crimes were only discovered by chance when police followed up the suicide of a suspect in the store theft. Leonard Lake had been arrested at the scene after his partner had dropped the stolen vice into their truck and then disappeared. A routine check on the vehicle by the responding officer had revealed that its number plates had been taken from a stolen Buick and that the identification documents that Lake had produced belonged to a far younger man, San Diego resident Robin Stapley. A search of the vehicle, a 1980 Honda, uncovered a .22 revolver fitted with a silencer. It was then confirmed that the gun was registered to Stapley, yet the large bearded man who claimed to be Stapley had informed the officer that the gun belonged to the owner of the Honda. If he was Stapley why would he claim that a licensed weapon belonged to another man whose car he had borrowed?

While the patrolman waited for an answer from headquarters, Lake produced a receipt to prove that he had paid for the vice that his friend had taken. But by now the officer was highly suspicious and was inclined to take him in for questioning. The Honda was impounded and an APB (all-points

> EVEN AS POLICE CLOSED IN ON THEIR CUSTOM-BUILT TORTURE CHAMBER, IT WAS ALREADY TOO LATE FOR AN ESTIMATED 25 VICTIMS

Leonard Lake (above) planned to create a new race by breeding with his captives; Ng was a fellow sexual sadist

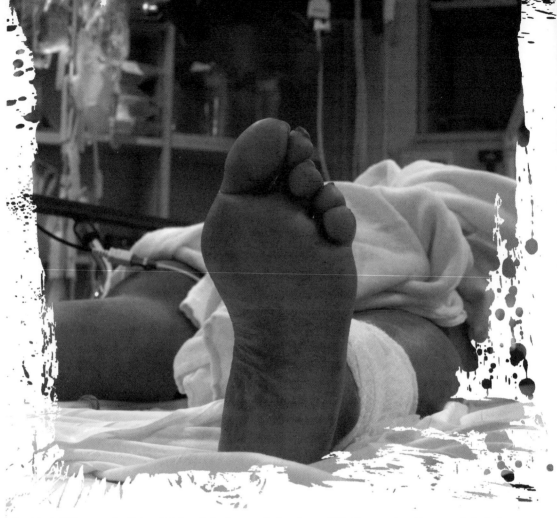

Leonard Lake was rushed to hospital where he lay in a coma for four days until his life support machine was switched off

bulletin) was issued for the arrest of Lake's accomplice, a slim dark-haired Asian male of about 25 years of age, wearing a parka.

At the police station Lake was asked to empty his pockets, which were found to contain a ticket issued to a Charles Gunnar.

When he was asked who Gunnar was and why he had a travel receipt belonging to another man, Lake looked uneasy and declined to answer. He was then told that the Honda was registered to a car dealer who had been listed as missing on 2 November 1984. Lake blanched and asked for a

glass of water and a pen and paper. His handcuffs were removed at his request and then he began scribbling a note he claimed was intended for his wife. He pocketed the message.

'I didn't think a lousy bench vice would bring me to this.'

Asked what he meant by that, Lake began what the officers hoped would be a confession, but his statement was brief: it still meant big trouble for the man whose identity he was revealing.

'My friend's name is Charlie Chitat Ng, Chitat, pronounced Cheetah and Ng, pronounced Ing.'

THE SUICIDE CLUE

He gave them his real name, Leonard Lake, and admitted that he was wanted by the FBI. But then he broke off. Pulling two capsules from under his lapel he popped them into his mouth and bit down on them, releasing the cyanide inside. He was rushed to hospital where he lay in a coma for four days until his life support machine was switched off. Leonard Lake had cheated the courts, but his partner was still on the run.

A death in custody demanded a serious investigation and a thorough examination of the impounded vehicle, which turned up two empty shell casings under the passenger seat, a bullet hole in the roof and bloodstains on the upholstery. Clearly the car itself was a crime scene and required a painstaking inspection. First of all, credit cards and documents bearing the name of Robin Stapley were found.

Lake had claimed to be Stapley when he was first arrested, yet it turned out that Stapley had been posted as missing. There was also a credit card issued to Randy Jacobsen and a gas and electricity bill addressed to Claralyn Balasz. All had to be checked out and accounted for. The bill was particularly interesting because enquiries revealed that Balasz was in fact Lake's former wife. She had been living in Wilseyville, California near the Sierra Nevada Mountains, more than 150 miles away, but had recently moved to San Bruno, just down the road from the South City store where Lake had been arrested.

On 3 June Balasz was interviewed by detectives from the Missing Persons Bureau, who asked her about her previous address in Wilseyville. She told them that it was a mountain cabin owned by her father in Calaveras County, which was too remote to be found without a guide.

When pressed, she volunteered to take them there the next day, when they were joined by Lake's mother Gloria Eberling, who seemed anxious to prevent the detectives from gaining access to the breeze block bunker without a warrant. The detectives were also surprised to see that it was just off Highway 88. They could have found it easily without help.

It did not take long for the detectives and the local sheriff to find incriminating evidence. There were faint blood stains on the living room ceiling and there was a bullet hole in the wall. Another bullet hole was found in the kitchen floor. More sinister items were to be seen in the main bedroom, where the four-poster bed was bolted to the floor and a floodlight had been installed on the far wall. Unusually the bed had two mattresses, with the lower one stained with what looked suspiciously like dried blood.

The detectives felt a sickening sense of unease

In a death reminiscent of Nazi leaders many years before, Lake swallowed his emergency cyanide capsules

when they noticed the electrical cables wrapped around each of the four posts and then discovered a collection of bloodstained women's underwear in a chest of drawers.

In the living room, a television and some audio duplicating equipment were identified as having been stolen from the home of the Dubs family, who had not been seen since 24 July the previous year. All of the serial numbers had been erased. The father, the mother and their baby son had vanished from their San Francisco home after being visited by two men, who had responded to an advertisement for audio-video equipment.

SECRETS OF THE BUNKER

A warrant to search the entire site was quickly obtained and the detectives returned to quiz the two women, who refused to co-operate with the investigation.

However, Balasz admitted that she had driven Charles Ng to the airport the previous day and that she had seen him pack a gun and ammunition as well as a significant amount of cash. She also mentioned that he possessed identification documents in the name of Mike Kimoto.

A warrant was issued for the detention of Ng, alias Kimoto, and then a 17-man task force descended on the Wilseyville site. Beginning on 4 June 1985 a painstaking search was made of the cabin, the bunker and an incinerator, as well as a trench and several mounds of earth in the vicinity. When shreds of clothing were found in the trench the Calaveras County sheriff decided that a search of the compound was necessary, so he enlisted the aid of a forensic pathologist and sniffer dogs.

Meanwhile, Sheriff Ballard and the two detectives who had conducted the initial investigation, Irene Brunn and Tom Eisenmann, entered the bunker where they found tools caked with dried blood.

The workshop was noticeably smaller on the inside than it had appeared on the outside which indicated that there was a concealed room. This was discovered behind a plywood tool rack. In the room they found a double bed, a shelf of survival handbooks and a small arsenal of weapons, including machine guns. A small window was fitted with a two-way mirror, giving the occupant a view of an inner chamber that was clearly fitted out like a cell to contain captives.

Little more evidence was needed to link Lake and Ng to the bodies that would soon be unearthed at the site. However, the forensic team also recovered the men's fingerprints from the two-way mirror and a handwritten diary detailing the rape and murder of the various victims. The diary also contained Lake's ravings on the subject of nuclear

> A SMALL WINDOW WAS FITTED WITH A TWO-WAY MIRROR, GIVING THE OCCUPANT A VIEW OF AN INNER CHAMBER FITTED OUT FOR CAPTIVES

war and his plan to create a new race by breeding with his captives.

It looked certain that the site would yield a considerable number of bodies, so before any serious excavation work was undertaken the FBI was alerted to the strong possibility that this could be a major murder investigation.

On the day that the digging equipment arrived detectives received an unexpected visitor in the form of Gloria Eberling, who had moderated her belligerent attitude and was now concerned about the fate of her other son, Donald, from whom she had not heard for two years. Her worst fears were soon to be confirmed.

As soon as the diggers began their work hundreds of incriminating items were unearthed, including clothing, wallets and documents. Then the first skeletal remains emerged, some of which had been dismembered and partially incinerated. There were also videotapes on which Lake and Ng could be seen abusing 18-year-old Kathleen Allen – whose boyfriend had been a cell mate of Charles Ng – and 19-year-old Brenda O'Connor, Lake's neighbour. Brenda was begging for the life of her baby, but the murderous pair had already killed the infant. Her partner Lonnie Bond, the baby's father, had also been reported missing.

It would eventually be possible to list Charles Ng's known victims as Kathleen Allen and her boyfriend Michael Carroll, Lonnie Bond and his baby son, also called Lonnie, Paul Cosner, Brenda O'Connor, Harvey and Deborah Dubs and their son Sean, Charles Gunnar (Lake's former friend), Randy Jacobsen, Donald Lake and Robin S. Stapley.

By the time the bunker had been demolished and the search had been concluded the remains of seven men, three women and two babies had been catalogued, together with a significant amount of assorted bone fragments.

All of this suggested that as many as 25 people might have met a terrible end at the site. But only 12 corpses could be positively identified from their dental and medical records, which meant that Charles Ng would be tried for the abduction and murder of 12 people.

DELAYING TACTICS

Justice finally caught up with Charles Ng in Calgary, Canada when he was arrested for shoplifting. He had stolen a few grocery items even though he had more than enough cash to pay for them. After a heated and protracted battle with the Canadian authorities, who were against extraditing suspects to any state that imposed the death penalty, he was transferred to Folsom Prison in Sacramento to stand trial. But in the six years it had taken to extradite him Ng had studied every American legal statute he could find and for the next 13 years he exploited every possible avenue of appeal to delay the only possible verdict.

Ng's trial finally began in October 1998. It was to last eight months, but it took the jury only a few hours to return a guilty verdict, with a recommendation that Ng be sentenced to death. The judge had the power to reduce the sentence to life, but in his summing-up he concurred with the jury. Having seen the videotapes and the damning forensic evidence, there was only one sentence that could be imposed. Charles Ng is currently appealing that sentence, a procedure which could last many more years. At time of writing, he is still on Death Row at San Quentin state prison.

KARLA HOMOLKA AND PAUL BERNARDO

When Paul and Karla Bernardo smiled for the photographer on the morning of their wedding they looked every inch the perfect couple. In fact, their blonde, blue-eyed good looks had earned them the nicknames 'Ken' and 'Barbie', because of their resemblance to the children's dolls of the same name. But their smiles hid the dark souls of two of America's most depraved and sadistic sex killers. Among their many female victims was Karla's own 15-year-old sister, Tammy Lyn, whose rape, torture and murder the couple would repeatedly re-enact, with Karla dressed in her dead sister's clothes.

Paul Kenneth Bernardo had already raped and terrorized seven women in the suburbs of Toronto, Canada. Why he felt the compulsion to force himself upon unwilling, defenceless girls, brutalizing and humiliating them, when he could have had a relationship with almost any woman he fancied is a mystery, but clearly he was incapable of developing a rapport with anyone other than a sadistic psychopathic personality like himself.

The Toronto attacks had becoming increasingly violent by 1988 and it was feared that the escalation would lead to murder, so the FBI was called in. The Canadian authorities had a vague description of the attacker, who was said to be handsome, fair-haired, slim and six foot tall. But there were no physical clues and there was no forensic evidence. Without a specimen of the offender's semen, hair, clothing fibres, footprints, blood or fingerprints, or a name, there was nothing

SMILES HID THE DARK SOULS OF TWO OF AMERICA'S MOST DEPRAVED AND SADISTIC SEX KILLERS. AMONG THEIR VICTIMS WAS KARLA'S OWN SISTER TAMMY LYN

Two of a kind: Karla could be heard encouraging Paul as she filmed him raping one of his victims

The rented house in St Catharines, Ontario where Karla's 15-year-old sister Tammy Lyn was raped and then died

to be gained from running a match. The only hope lay in narrowing down the list of suspects by compiling a psychological profile.

PROFILING A KILLER

The job was assigned to two of the FBI's most experienced men, special agents John Douglas and Gregg McCrary, who were based at the Behavioral Science Unit at Quantico, Virginia. When Douglas and McCrary surveyed the crime scenes and read the witnesses' statements they were able to draw a number of conclusions. The first one was that the 'UNSUB', or unknown subject, was most likely a local man living with his parents. All of the attacks had occurred in Scarborough, a

middle-class neighbourhood, where a single man could not afford to purchase a home of his own. And the crime scenes formed a cluster. If the rapist had followed the victims from the centre of Toronto to Scarborough he would not have ended up attacking them within a few miles of each other. So he and his victims all came from the same area. And all but one of his victims were attacked from behind, presumably to minimize the risk of being recognized. It was also known that serial rapists tend to operate within a comfort zone, a familiar environment where they can stalk their victims and then follow a number of escape routes to their home.

His loathing for women would be known to

his family or his friends because suppressed aggression of the intensity that erupts into violence cannot be contained indefinitely. At some point the UNSUB must have let his hatred for women slip out before he could stop himself and someone must have remembered a shocking incident like that.

In their report, Douglas and McCrary observed the development of sadistic tendencies, for example when the rapist asked the seventh victim the question, 'Should I kill you?', which prompted her to beg for her life. According to their report,

'The sadist achieves gratification by the victim's response to his attempts to dominate and control her either physically or psychologically, by posing a question that made the victim beg for her life he is deriving pleasure.'

The report concluded with a warning.

'The nature of these attacks will continue to be episodic and sporadic... Each attack is precipitated by a stressor in the offender's life. This stressor could be either one in fact or in his mind.... Your offender harbours no guilt or remorse for these *crimes. He believes his anger is justified and, therefore, so are the resultant attacks. His only concern is being identified and apprehended.'*

TRAPPED BY A LOVERS' SPAT

By the spring of 1991 the file on the Scarborough rapist had doubled in size. It included the details of 15 attacks and yet more witness statements, but no clues. The investigators could only hope that the perpetrator would make a slip so that he could be caught in the act. That summer, FBI agent McCrary returned to Canada to investigate the murder of two teenage girls in the Toronto area. He was soon speculating that the murders could be connected with the unsolved series of rapes in Scarborough.

The two killings did not at first seem to be connected because the first victim, 14-year-old Leslie Mahaffy, had been dismembered, whereas the second, 15-year-old Kristen French, had not. And Mahaffy had been abducted in the daytime, murdered, covered in concrete and submerged in a lake, while French was kidnapped after dark and her body was left in the open. Both, though, had been sexually assaulted and suffocated and both bore almost identical pressure marks on their

> DOUGLAS AND MCCRARY OBSERVED THE DEVELOPMENT OF SADISTIC TENDENCIES, FOR EXAMPLE WHEN THE RAPIST ASKED THE VICTIM, 'SHOULD I KILL YOU?'

backs. The killer had presumably knelt on them when strangling them from behind.

But the most curious fact linking the two killings was that the first girl had been abducted in Burlington and her body deposited in St Catharine's, whereas the second girl had been dumped in Burlington after having been snatched from the streets of St Catharine's.

The link was too significant to discount as mere coincidence. Moreover, McCrary was aware that the perpetrator in both rapes and killings was a sadistic sex offender and that only two per cent of violent offenders fall into this category. The chances of more than one individual operating in the same area were too remote. It had to be the same person. What the FBI and the other investigators did not know, and could not have known, was that the serial rapist and murderer had a partner. It was only when the pair had a lovers' spat that the truth finally came out.

On 5 January 1993 Karla Homolka was treated for injuries inflicted by her husband, who had beaten her with a flashlight during a violent argument. Karla was so incensed that she wanted to file charges. When the local police arrived at her aunt and uncle's house to interview her they brought another pair of officers, who were introduced as being from the Toronto Sexual Assault Squad. DNA tests had been made on semen recovered from a rape victim in 1990 and it had taken over two years to obtain samples from over 200 men in the area and then identify the source. The forensic laboratory had named Karla's husband, Paul, as the rapist and now there was reason to suspect that Paul might have been involved in the murder of the two teenage girls. If she had anything to tell them, now would be a good time.

CAUGHT ON CAMERA

Karla played the role of the battered wife convincingly. In July 1993, before the full extent of her part in the murders became known, she was able to secure a guarantee of complete immunity from the Canadian Department of Justice. If any of the detectives had doubted that such an attractive young woman could be capable of active participation in sadistic sex murders they had their preconceptions shattered after viewing the videotapes that the pair had made of their

KARLA CONSIDERED HER PARTICIPATION IN THE RAPE OF HER SISTER, 15-YEAR-OLD TAMMY LYN, TO BE HER CHRISTMAS PRESENT TO PAUL

crimes. The tapes had been hidden in the couple's rented house in Port Dalhousie and they made sickening viewing. Karla had filmed at least one of the Scarborough rapes and she could be heard encouraging her husband from behind the camera.

But even more shocking was the fact that the tapes recorded the torture and murder of victims who were unknown to the police. One of these was Karla's sister, 15-year-old Tammy Lyn. Karla considered her participation in the rape of Tammy Lyn to be her Christmas present to Paul. She supplied the drugs to sedate her sister and when he had finished she took over, sexually abusing the unconscious girl for their mutual pleasure. The camcorder was still running when Tammy choked and her attackers could not revive her. At the time the pathologist had found no evidence of foul play and so the police had concluded that the girl's death had been a tragic accident resulting from a drug overdose. But the video proved otherwise.

Paul Bernardo's pleasant persona was also a sham. Former girlfriends told detectives that at first he would be considerate and polite, but once he was confident that the girl was infatuated with him he would become abusive. He could only be sexually aroused when he was inflicting pain and he had a compulsion to dominate, control and humiliate his lovers.

Paul had groomed his former girlfriends to satisfy his sadistic fantasies. He had restricted their access to their families, chosen their clothes and flattered them to wear down their resistance to his demands. Their compliance and dependency only reinforced his contempt for them.

Then he attempted to do the same with Karla, who was just 17 years old when they met. She did more than share his fantasies, though, because she was willing to participate in the abuse of other women. On the day of her sister's funeral Karla dressed in the dead girl's clothes and then made a video of herself, in which she promised to procure young girls for her husband's entertainment. His look of surprise, captured on camera, seemed genuine. Karla appeared to have instigated the abductions of Kristen French and Leslie Mahaffy. And it was clear that she had not filmed their deaths against her will, as claimed. The excerpt showing Kristen screaming for help while Paul raped her was recorded by someone who held the camera with steady hands. FBI agent McCrary described her as a 'truly deviant personality'.

When faced with the forensic evidence and the videotapes, Karla expressed no remorse. She shared her husband's view that their victims had been objects to be used and abused. Karla and Paul were as unfeeling as the Ken and Barbie dolls they resembled.

In May 1995 Paul Bernardo was found guilty of first degree murder, kidnapping, sexual assault and forcible confinement, for which he received a mandatory life sentence. He will be eligible for parole in 2020.

The deal Karla had made with the Canadian Department of Justice did not mean that she would walk free, only that she would not be tried for murder. At her trial she was convicted on the lesser count of manslaughter. She was sentenced to two consecutive 10-year terms for her part in the killing of French and Mahaffy, with an additional two years for conspiring to cover up the facts relating to her sister's death. She was denied parole in 1997 and again in 2001.

BETTER A BAD MAN THAN NO MAN AT ALL –
FROGGIE AND MICKIE

Much has been written on the subject of criminal profiling and numerous theories have been offered to account for the aberrant behaviour of serial killers, who have been afforded a perverse form of celebrity status by our media-centred society. Clues to their sadistic compulsions are sought in their childhood and traumatic events in their lives are eagerly identified as the 'stressors' that set them off on their killing sprees. But many people have suffered rejection in their relationships, or have experienced bullying at school or the trauma of divorce, and yet they have still managed to keep their regrets, resentments and other personal feelings in check. And, conversely, not all serial killers conform to the typical or standard profile.

James Anthony Daveggio, the Californian serial rapist and sex killer who converted his minivan into a mobile torture chamber, had not wet his his bed, tortured animals or set fire to property. Nor had he suffered from a head injury, physical disfigurement or abuse as a child. According to the criteria of criminal psychology he was alternately an organized and a disorganized lust killer, which means that he planned some of his offences while other attacks were opportunistic. Moreover, a psychiatric report that was compiled following his arrest for the sexual assault of six women and the murder of two more concluded that he was clinically sane and fit to stand trial. It seems that Daveggio and his equally depraved female partner Michelle 'Mickie' Michaud were simply oversexed, sadistic degenerates who had no self-control and no empathy for those they chose to inflict their sick fantasies upon.

THE MAKING OF A MURDERER

It is believed that Daveggio might have claimed his first victim in 1974 at the tender age of 14.

JAMES DAVEGGIO AND MICHELLE MICHAUD WERE SIMPLY OVERSEXED, SADISTIC DEGENERATES WHO HAD NO SELF-CONTROL

'Froggie' drifted into petty crime at a young age; 'Mickie' was a prostitute who shared his sadomasochistic fantasies

Evil makeover: Daveggio joined the 'Devil's Horsemen', stole a Harley-Davidson, dyed his hair and had his arms tattooed

At that time he was one of a number of teenage boys questioned about the disappearance of 13-year-old Cassie Riley, whose partially clothed body was found on an embankment. Among other things, detectives noted the imprints of a pair of size 10 sneakers. There was no evidence of rape, but the victim had been beaten and then drowned in the creek. This suggested that her attacker had tried to force himself on her but when he had failed to perform he had lashed out and killed her. Witnesses reported seeing her talking with an older boy, who was wearing a green shirt with a patch on the sleeve. Daveggio was one of several boys interviewed, but another boy was eventually accused of the crime. However, Daveggio's sister later claimed that her mother had lied about his whereabouts to give him an alibi. Whatever the truth, he was then forgotten. Had he been formally questioned it might have put the brakes on his descent into even more serious crime.

Daveggio was brought up by his mother after his parents divorced. Without a father to set him straight he drifted into petty crime, stealing cars and fighting. Tired of hauling him out of trouble his mother sent him to live with his father in Pacifica, California but that did not work out. Jim's hard-drinking dad was no role model so the boy was sent back to his mother. He continued to reoffend. His activities escalated to robbery, which earned him his first spell in the Alameda

County boy's detention camp — where he picked up the nickname 'Froggie', together with a lifelong addiction to gambling and popping pills. On his release he proved to be a poster boy for the three-strikes-and-you're-out campaign by continually forcing himself on young girls, whom he had plied with liquor so that they could not cry rape. Although none of his predatory sexual assaults landed him in court, they were sufficiently serious to require him to submit to a psychiatric evaluation. It was decided that he was a sex offender who required treatment at the California Medical Facility in Vacaville. It was a short vacation for Daveggio, who celebrated his release by propositioning a female officer posing as a prostitute. He was driving under the influence of alcohol at the time.

With such a bulging young offender's record, Daveggio thought it might be wise to drop below the radar by moving to Sacramento, where in 1997 he joined a motorcycle gang known as the 'Devil's Horsemen'. The only problem was that he did not own a motorbike — but he knew someone who did, so he stole his. Then he dyed his hair and had his arms tattooed. With his new image, and a Harley-Davidson to impress the gang and their girls, he prowled the neighbourhood until he picked up prostitute Michelle 'Mickie' Michaud, who shared his sadomasochistic fantasies.

SINISTER ROLE MODEL

He moved in with her and played 'daddy' to her daughters, but he had other games in mind. At first he enjoyed humiliating Mickie by complaining about whatever she did and treating her like a whore. Then he began bringing other women home and beating her when she protested. After being fired from his job as a barman, on suspicion of having robbed the safe, he turned to drug dealing. He sold crack cocaine from the house, which brought him to the attention of the police. When they discovered that he was a registered sex offender who was living in a house where there were children, they ordered him to move out. Even the motorcycle gang disowned him. It was at this point that he became obsessed with serial killers and decided that he wanted a share of their notoriety and 'the thrill of the kill'.

He modelled himself on killer Gerald Gallego, who had convinced his partner Charlene to procure a victim for him to molest and murder. Gallego felt that young girls would be wary of being approached by a man, but he knew they could be persuaded to go with a woman, even if

> HE SOLD CRACK COCAINE FROM THE HOUSE WHICH BROUGHT HIM TO THE ATTENTION OF POLICE. WHEN THEY DISCOVERED HE WAS A REGISTERED SEX OFFENDER, THEY ORDERED HIM TO MOVE OUT

she was a stranger to them. Inspired by Gallego's example, Daveggio told Mickie to entice one of his daughter's friends to his house, where he would rape her. Once Mickie had proved herself to be a willing accomplice the pair set out on a hunt for victims. Twenty-year-old student Alicia Paredes was the first to be snatched off the street as she was walking home one evening. She was bundled into the van and driven to a remote location where she was raped – but she was allowed to live. It suited the couple's perverted power game to show mercy when it suited them. In this instance it was a fatal mistake because Alicia was able to tell the police that she remembered the man calling his female accomplice 'Mickie'. This detail was added to their file, together with a police artist's sketch of the couple drawn to match Alicia's description.

But it was not enough to save other girls from a similar fate. The next victim was forced to perform oral sex on 'Daddy' Daveggio, while Mickie held her down. A surfeit of booze and pills was making Daveggio lose his grip on reality, because he tried to comfort the girl after her ordeal and even sent Mickie to buy ice to soothe her injuries. He clearly had no grasp of the trauma he had subjected her to and must have imagined that he only had to console her to make everything all right again. He had depersonalized her, but in his self-centred world she was merely an object to gratify his desires and her pain was an inconvenience comparable with the needs of a demanding pet dog.

The pair's depravity reached a new low with their sexual assault on Mickie's daughter a few days later. Even her own offspring's pleading failed to move the psychotic woman, who held her down

while Daveggio had oral sex with her. Some time later, still untroubled by their consciences, or even by the fear of being caught, the pair lured another female victim into the minivan with the promise of cocaine. Then they hit her over the head and demanded that she submit to degrading acts with Daveggio. But when the sobbing girl told them that the experience reminded her of what had happened with her stepfather, Daveggio lost interest. Mickie was not so easily turned off, however. She molested the girl and then took photographs, threatening to blackmail her if she went to the police.

THE TORTURE WAGON

In early November Mickie was arrested for passing bad cheques, so she spent a short time in jail. While she was there Daveggio finished converting their vehicle. He kitted it out with ropes and chains to make his fantasy of a mobile torture wagon a reality.

THE PAIR'S DEPRAVITY REACHED A NEW LOW WITH THEIR SEXUAL ASSAULT ON MICKIE'S DAUGHTER A FEW DAYS LATER

Hunting ground: the area round Sacramento was no longer safe for women when Froggie and Mickie were on the prowl

As soon as Mickie was out the twosome resumed their 'adventures', but the next victim wriggled free and escaped. She was then able to give information to the police, which was backed up by statements from Daveggio's daughter and a friend of Mickie's daughter.

This put the police on the couple's trail, but they did not close in fast enough. Daveggio turned on his own daughter in a Sacramento motel. He raped her for a while and then Mickie joined in. When they were done he told his daughter that he wanted to torture her, but she threatened to scream for help so he promised to find someone else.

On the morning of 2 December Daveggio and Mickie were cruising around the California suburb of Pleasanton, eyeing up potential victims, when Daveggio picked 'the one with the pretty black hair'. He had chosen 22-year-old Vanessa Lei Samson, who was taking her regular walk to work. Two workmen on a nearby roof heard a piercing scream and the door of a van sliding shut. When they looked down they noticed a dark green minivan being driven by a woman. They assumed it was a mother and daughter arguing so they did not report it until the police asked for witnesses to the abduction.

Vanessa was gagged with a sex toy bought from a local store and then tortured with curling irons. When Daveggio had finished with her, he swapped places with Mickie and then drove to a hotel in

Lake Tahoe is a famous beauty spot, but Daveggio and Michaud didn't go there to admire the views

South Lake Tahoe, where they smuggled the girl into their room and subjected her to a prolonged and agonizing assault.

The last thing Vanessa ever heard was Daveggio's voice telling her that they were going to be 'bonded forever'.

As he said those words, he tightened a rope round her neck and strangled her. The couple dumped her body 30 feet down an embankment in Alpine County and then returned to their motel, which was also in Tahoe.

DAVEGGIO'S DAUGHTER TESTIFIES

The next day, 3 December 1997, Mickie was due in court on the bad cheque charge but she did not turn up, so the police called at her home and talked her mother into revealing her whereabouts. They took the couple into custody without a struggle, but at this time they had no idea that the pair had committed anything more serious than fraud. However, Mickie had boasted about her role in Vanessa Lei's murder to her cellmate, who reported the incident to detectives. It was then that they looked more closely at the items recovered from the van. These included a dated receipt from a Pleasanton motel, which linked the suspects with the crime scene, and the gag that contained traces of Vanessa's saliva. Detectives now realized that they were holding a serial killer or killers.

A grand jury was summoned to determine whether there was sufficient evidence to commit the accused to trial. During the hearing Daveggio's 16-year-old daughter testified that on Thanksgiving Day 1997 her father had asked her if she wanted to join him in a 'hunt' for a victim.

'He told me I would never know if I'd like killing someone unless I had tried,' she said.

He had also sought her reassurance that if he did kill someone he could count on her to hide him out. The reluctant teenager was then browbeaten by Mickie Michaud, who could barely contain her excitement at the thought of kidnapping someone they would have at their mercy.

'Michelle told me (that the day after Thanksgiving) was the biggest shopping day of the year and would be the best day to go kill somebody... She tried to get me to go with her and my dad. But I wasn't going with them.'

In sentencing Daveggio and Michaud to death Judge

Larry Goodman cited 'overwhelming and undisputed' evidence of their guilt. He described the murder of Vanessa Samson as 'vile, cruel, senseless, depraved, brutal, evil and vicious'. His comments were echoed by Deputy District Attorney Angela Backers for the prosecution, who said that the case was unique in the annals of Alameda County, being an example of 'pure evil and utter depravity'. Michaud had described each vicious assault as an 'adventure', and Daveggio had referred to them as 'huntings'.

'These two defendants are simply the worst of the worst,' Backers declared.

Prior to the sentencing of the couple, the Samson family were allowed to address Daveggio, who remained unmoved and again denied that he had been responsible for the death of Vanessa Lei. Her mother, Christina, told the court that she cries every day for the loss of her daughter, reserving her grief for the early morning hours when the rest of the family are asleep and cannot hear her. What makes her loss all the more unbearable is knowing that her daughter was tortured and assaulted. 'She was in terror. Frightened beyond words,' Christina Samson told the court. 'She was brutally tortured and she was defenseless and alone... With the murder of my Vanessa Lei, a part of me died.'

DEATH IN THE DESERT –

DAVID RAY AND CYNTHIA HENDY

They called it their 'Toy Box', but the contents of the trailer owned by David Parker Ray and Cynthia (Cindy) Lea Hendy spelt fun only for them. For their victims it meant a living hell of sexual degradation and unbearable pain.

Few serial killers express genuine remorse, if only because their psychosis has developed from a lack of empathy and their inability to identify with the anguish of others. Those who do come to realize the enormity of the suffering they have caused often turn to religion to assuage their guilt and try to distance themselves from the actions inflicted by their 'former' selves. But many continue to revel in the power they held over their helpless victims and glory in the publicity they attract from a horrified but fascinated public. David Parker Ray fitted into the last category. He feigned guilt, but he was beyond redemption.

OUT OF NOWHERE

She came running barefoot from the desert on to the highway. No one stopped, even though she was crying for help and waving her arms. She almost threw herself in front of one car, but the driver swerved to avoid her and then accelerated, cursing as he cast a glance into the rear-view mirror. All he could see was a naked girl wearing a metal collar and chain, her mouth frozen into a scream, her hair and face spattered with blood like an extra from *The Texas Chainsaw Massacre*.

And then she saw the trailers squatting in the

ALL HE COULD SEE WAS A NAKED GIRL WEARING A METAL COLLAR AND CHAIN, HER MOUTH FROZEN IN A SCREAM, HER HAIR AND FACE SPATTERED WITH BLOOD

Ray revelled in the power he held over helpless victims; Hendy was his willing accomplice

'Help me, help me': Cynthia Vigil came running out of the desert on to the highway and desperately tried to flag cars down

rippling desert haze beneath the Sierra Caballo mountains. She beat her fists on one and then another, but no one answered. Then the door of the third mobile home swung open and the girl pulled herself inside. There she came face to face with a startled old woman who nevertheless had the presence of mind to wrap the naked girl in a blanket and call the police.

The date was 22 March 1999 and it was almost dusk. When the police arrived, the traumatized girl could only repeat her name, Cynthia Vigil, and cry, 'I'm alive! I'm alive!'

When she had calmed down enough to tell her story, she described her kidnap in Albuquerque three days earlier. A man and a woman had held her captive in a mobile home and proceeded to torture her. She had been touting for business as a hooker and the man had offered to pay her for sex in his car.

FAKE COP

Her instincts told her she was in deep trouble when she climbed into the Toyota and saw another woman, but when the man pulled out a police badge and told her they were taking her in for soliciting she did not resist. It was only when they drove out of town that she realized that this was one trick she might not live through.

Luckily, she managed to escape when the man went to work and the woman left the keys to her chains within reach. Cynthia freed herself and dialled 911 before the woman could stop her. There was a struggle, the call was cut off and a box of torture instruments was sent crashing to the ground, its contents spilling. One of these was a lethal-looking ice pick, which Cynthia instinctively grabbed and thrust into her jailer's neck. But she had neither the strength nor the will to finish her tormentor off. Her only thought was of escape.

No one who looked at her injuries could have doubted her story. Her body was tattooed with bruises, welts and electrical burns and her breasts were covered in vicious-looking punctures. Even though the New Mexico patrolmen had lost no time in reporting in, other officers were already at the crime scene. They too had responded to the aborted emergency call. Some of the officers were checking out a trailer home that was parked at 513 Bass Road, overlooking a reservoir in the resort of Elephant Butte. What they found there sickened even the most experienced officers.

The owners of the trailer were apprehended as they were attempting to flee the scene in their Toyota RV (recreational vehicle). It was the car in which Cynthia's abductors had been travelling. If her story was true the vehicle would contain evidence such as blood and hair as well as fingerprints. The car was impounded so that an inch-by-inch search could be made by forensic officers, but a cursory glance was enough to justify the arrest of its owners. It had been kitted out to look like an official police vehicle, which in itself was against the law, and a restraining clamp had been fixed to the back seat, which was certainly not standard police practice.

THE 'TOY BOX' IS OPENED

Meanwhile the driver, 59-year-old David Ray, and his girlfriend, 39-year-old Cindy Hendy, were handcuffed and taken in for questioning. It was clear that they had been rehearsing, because their stories were eerily similar in so many respects. According to them, Cynthia was a heroin addict whose alleged experiences were nothing more than the memory of a bad trip. They had been trying to help her kick the addiction by confining her for her own good. Her injuries had been sustained when they had tried to restrain her. The detectives dutifully recorded these statements without comment, but they gave them no credibility whatsoever. They recognized a victim of violence when they saw one and they could also tell when they were being fed a string of lies by a pathological liar. The results of the forensic tests would provide all the proof they needed.

When they searched the trailer, the detectives discovered the fake police badge that Ray had used to con his victims. They also found his handwritten notes to Hendy, in which he told her how to deal with their captives if they got restless. Even more damning was an audio tape he had recorded. Played to each new victim, it described the programme of torture he planned for them and how they were to behave if they wanted to survive. This included calling him 'master' and his accomplice 'mistress'. If the victims hesitated, or refused to join in the planned 'games', they would be severely punished. The couple had also videoed a 'session' in which a victim was strapped into a gynaecology chair and forced to watch her own torment on a monitor. The officers who viewed this material later admitted that it was among the worst crimes they had ever witnessed.

Parked alongside the first trailer was a smaller one, which was designed for storage or transporting bulky items. This was the torture chamber that Ray and Hendy called their 'Toy Box'. It was stacked with surgical instruments, sadomasochistic restraints, cattle prods, stun guns, whips and all manner of hellish implements. Ray was methodical in his madness and would constantly refer to a collection of medical manuals in order to gain ideas on how to administer the most intense agony.

Everything Ray had inflicted on the women had been planned and recorded in a journal. He had made drawings in advance of what he intended to do to them and had dressed dolls in sadomasochistic gear to feed his fantasies. He had also taken photographs of the 'operations' he had performed on his 'packages', to savour at a later date. He knew exactly what he was doing. If he had intended to plead insanity he had already undermined his case by recording the 16 methods he had devised for conditioning sex slaves. They included rewarding compliance and cultivating their dependency on their 'dungeon master'. The list was irrefutable proof that Ray was fully aware of his actions.

A SURVIVOR COMES FORWARD

Nevertheless, the authorities were worried that a jury might dismiss the charges if it thought prostitute Cynthia Vigil might have been a willing victim. What they desperately needed was to locate another survivor who would be willing to testify.

Fortunately the publicity surrounding Ray and Hendy's arrest had reached the neighbouring town of Truth or Consequences, where resident Angelica Montano had been hoping to put her ordeal at the hands of the psychotic couple behind her. But the appeal for witnesses, and the thought that the duo might get away with it if no one came forward, was enough for Angelica to overcome her fear and help the prosecution.

She gave a statement to the police in which she described how she was abducted at gunpoint on 17 February, after calling on the couple to ask if they had some cooking ingredients. They strapped her to an obstetrics table, subjected her to electric shocks and penetrated her violently with sex toys while she begged them to stop. Then on the fourth day they drove her out to a remote spot in the desert and left her there to die. But a passing patrol car came by just in time and she was taken to hospital. Incredibly, her complaint was never pursued and no reasons were given for the failure to follow up.

The woman in the video was eventually identified and interviewed, but her recollection of

The 'Toy Box' was a mobile torture chamber containing surgical instruments and all manner of hellish implements

the horrific events was so vague that her statement was of little use to the police. She had apparently been drugged by Ray and Hendy in 1996. However, she managed to itemize the contents of the 'Toy Box', which was of help in building the case against the duo.

THE SUSPECTS

When Cindy Hendy was interviewed she told detectives she was a mother of three from Seattle who had left her children because she suffered from manic depression and was going to be charged for drug possession, forgery and theft. She knew she was implicated in one of the most heinous kidnapping and torture cases of recent times and was more than anxious to tell all she knew in exchange for a lesser sentence. In particular, she was keen to distance herself from

several murders that Ray had committed to hide his crimes. However, she hinted that as many as 14 bodies were to be found. Six of them had been dismembered and dropped into Elephant Butte Lake after Ray had slit them open at the stomach to ensure they did not float back to the surface.

In exchange for a 36-year sentence she also offered up Ray's daughter, Glenda Jean 'Jesse' Ray, as a former partner in the torture murders and said that a local man, Dennis Roy Yancy, was also involved. She claimed he had taken part in the killing of a young mother of two, Marie B. Parker.

When Yancy was brought in he confirmed that he and Jesse Ray had watched the torture and rape of Marie Parker, but that she had been a willing participant. In fact, she had been his girlfriend. On 5 July 1997 he procured her for the pleasure of David Ray, but when he saw her being led to the

The New Mexico state police display the terrible contraption that was found in David Ray's trailer

car in handcuffs he feared she would be killed and was tempted to call the police. However, he claimed that he had been afraid of Ray and so he had done nothing until the couple told him that they were done with the girl. He was then ordered to strangle her and help dispose of her body. When the case reached court Yancy received two sentences of 15 years to run consecutively, which meant that he would remain in prison for 30 years.

In March 2000 the proceedings against David Ray did not go so smoothly. His trial for the kidnapping and assault of Cynthia Vigil was due to take place in Tierra Amarilla, New Mexico, but he delayed it by feigning a heart attack. The judge put the trial on hold when he realized that changing dates would make it difficult to call several key witnesses. Instead, he brought forward an entirely different case – that of Kelly Van Cleave, the woman who had been kidnapped and videotaped in 1996. However, her recollection of events was no less vague than before and it had been distorted by the drugs she had been given. The prosecution case was made even weaker by the judge's decision to exclude Ray's written list of procedures for conditioning a slave. He also barred any reference to torture instruments, on the grounds that they might not have been the ones that were discovered in the trailer at the time of Ray's arrest!

EVADING JUSTICE

And then came tragedy when prosecution witness Angelica Montano died at the age of 25. The case collapsed and the judge was forced to order the restart of the first trial, even though the prosecution case was not as strong as it would have been some months earlier. This trial was to prove a bad day for justice. The jury was divided between those who found the chief witness, Kelly Van Cleave, credible and those who doubted her story. Efforts were made to attribute the inconsistencies in her statements to the drugs she had been given, but not everyone was convinced. Even so, the prosecution was confident that the forensic evidence would tell its own story. However, after the closing arguments had been made the jury was unable to agree on a verdict, which forced the judge to declare a mistrial. Afterwards one of the jurors told journalists that he could not be sure that the girl had been unwilling. Some people like rough sex, he told them.

The witness was distraught when she heard the verdict and she was even more unnerved by the possibility that she would have to relive her ordeal all over again at the retrial. But the retrial focused on the charges relating to the kidnapping and rape of Angelica Montano and this time the new jury returned a guilty verdict.

Realizing that his goose was cooked, Ray cut a deal shortly after the next trial began. He agreed to plead guilty to the abduction, rape and torture of Cynthia Vigil and another unnamed woman in exchange for leniency for his daughter. That landed him with a 233-year stretch. His daughter Glenda (Jesse) received a six-year suspended sentence for aiding and abetting in a kidnap plus five years to be served on probation. It was an empty gesture of magnanimity by Ray. He showed his true, devious nature only days later by appealing his sentence on the grounds that he had been exhausted and ill at the time and his judgment had been 'clouded' by medication.

It was a cynical ploy and one that cut no ice with the three judges, who threw out the appeal with a note to the effect that the accused had been on normal medication at the time and could not produce an expert witness to argue otherwise.

Ray once boasted that he had killed one person every year for the past 40 years, but police believe this was just another sick fantasy. No bodies were ever found relating to the case, not even those which Hendy claimed had been submerged in the lake. But that did not diminish the crimes for which she and Ray were imprisoned – kidnap, torture and rape.

Then on 28 May 2002 David Parker Ray suffered a genuine heart attack at the Lea County Correctional Facility and died aged 62. The news gave no satisfaction to his surviving victims, who must have longed to see him suffer as much and for as long as they had.

'I can only be sorry for what I did,' he said.

This was neither an apology nor an admission of guilt, but merely a reflection of his own inability to care what happened to those whose lives he had destroyed in the most heinous way imaginable.

CHAPTER 5

IT COULD HAPPEN ANYWHERE

Serial killers are not an exclusively American phenomenon, although the media often give the impression that the US is seething with chainsaw-wielding psychopaths and sinister neighbours who have built a torture chamber in their suburban cellar. Murder is a universal scourge and every country has its share of deadly duos who labour under the delusion that they are above the law or too clever to be caught. Fortunately, few manage to escape justice for ever.

INDIA'S CAUSE CÉLÈBRE –

DR HENRY CLARK AND AUGUSTA FULHAM

India is infested with poisonous snakes, none more deadly than the human variety. Some blame the stifling heat, others the exotic setting for the strange effect the subcontinent had on its white colonial inhabitants in the days of the Raj. Many prim upper-class ladies and starch-collared gentlemen lost their inhibitions when the sun went down. One fatally affected fellow was Dr Henry Clark, who blamed the murder of his wife on the 'thugees', a fanatical cult who worshipped Kali, the eight-armed goddess of death. Dr Clark had a cast-iron alibi, which placed him several miles away at the time of the killing in March 1913 and in full view of several reliable witnesses. But there were rumours that the good doctor had been guilty of conduct unbecoming a gentleman when he had pursued a relationship with a married woman, Mrs Augusta Fulham.

The rumours were well founded because the

Kali is the many-armed goddess of death, who perhaps gained too much control over Dr Henry Clark

THE LETTERS REVEALED DETAILS OF A PLOT: DR CLARK SUPPLIED THE ARSENIC POWDER AND AUGUSTA ADMINISTERED IT

Days of the British Raj: beneath the thin veneer of respectability there was a hidden world of intrigue

police found almost 400 letters from Dr Clark to Mrs Fulham when they searched the lady's home in Agra. The letters did not only contain words of love – they also revealed the details of a plot to poison the unsuspecting Mr Fulham. Dr Clark supplied the arsenic powder and Augusta administered it. When her husband complained of stomach cramps he was taken to hospital, where Dr Clark finished him off with a second dose. The thugees, it transpired, had been paid by Dr Clark to remove his wife from the scene so that he could be comforted in his bereavement by the young widow. The couple would then arouse little suspicion when they married. Sadly, the only solemn vows Dr Clark made were to the priest who accompanied him to the gallows on 26 March 1913. Fulham was spared the noose because she was pregnant at the time of her trial, but she was given a life sentence in one of India's most formidable prisons. Mercifully, she died of heatstroke the following year.

THE PUPPET MASTER –
WERNER BOOST
AND FRANZ LORBACH

In the chaos of post-war Germany many murders went undetected and unsolved. It was open season for serial killers, who could settle old scores or simply hunt for 'sport', secure in the knowledge that their killings would be attributed to the Russian invaders or desperate German deserters. No one had the resources, the energy or the inclination to investigate civilian deaths. Germany was a country overrun with refugees, liberated prisoners and 'displaced persons', all without identification documents.

Werner Boost had acquired a taste for killing in the war and found he could satisfy his bloodlust shooting refugees

At Helmstedt, in Lower Saxony, several refugees had been shot as they attempted to escape from the Russian zone, but not by the sentries who patrolled the new border. They were the first victims of former German conscript Werner Boost, who had acquired a taste for killing in the final year of the war and now found that he could satisfy his bloodlust by targeting fleeing refugees as they raced across the open fields to freedom in the West. It was like shooting rabbits, only the thrill was more intense. And it was addictive.

The war did not make Werner a murderer – he had displayed a mean streak even in childhood, for by the age of six he had been convicted of theft and sent to a home for delinquent boys in Magdeburg. However, when the Russians reinforced their patrols along the border at Helmstedt he abandoned his hunting to concentrate on stealing scrap metal from graveyards. After all, there was no money to be made from shooting refugees who had nothing but the clothes on their back.

But in 1951 he was caught and sent to prison. On his release he met a simple-minded and gullible soul named Franz Lorbach, who believed Werner's heroic war stories and became his trusting sidekick. Like the somnambulistic Cesare in the German impressionist film *The Cabinet of*

Police investigate the site of a double murder, later attributed to Boost, in a field in Lower Büderich, near Düsseldorf

Dr. Caligari, Lorbach submitted to the will of his domineering partner by aiding him in the robbery and murder of courting couples, who always chose remote locations and did not put up any resistance. Werner held them at gunpoint while Franz drugged them with a concoction his master had created. Then with their victims sedated Werner would shoot the man and rape the woman, before killing her too. If they found money or other valuables on their victims, that would be a bonus.

But they had not planned for the unexpected. One night in 1956 they came across two male lovers. Dr Serve from Düsseldorf and his male friend were sharing an intimate moment when they were accosted by Werner and Franz. Werner did not wait to administer the drug but shot the doctor without thinking and then ordered Franz to kill the man's companion. But Franz bungled it, which enabled the young man to give detectives a detailed description of his attackers.

However, the killings continued. The next couple were murdered with a bullet to the head and cyanide before being partially burned near the scene and two further victims were drowned in a lake in their own car after being knocked unconscious. But it was the last thrill that Werner would enjoy at someone else's expense. On 6 June 1956 a labourer saw him spying on a courting couple. The man tackled him and alerted the lovers, who sent for the police. When Franz read about Werner's arrest in the morning paper he walked into the local police station and made a full and detailed confession. His 'master' was sentenced to life imprisonment.

THE PRIVILEGED PSYCHOS –

MARIO FURLAN AND WOLFGANG ABEL

Some people can be too clever for their own good. When an uncommonly high level of intelligence is combined with an oversized ego, money to burn and time to kill, a potentially lethal cocktail is created. Add in a fatal psychological flaw – the inability to tell the difference between right and wrong – and the mixture becomes explosive. If such people have been raised on the idea that their privileged background sets them above the law, it will only be a matter of time before they test their 'superior' intellect against the simple deductive reasoning practised by the police.

Italian Mario Furlan and his German friend Wolfgang Abel were the sons of wealthy parents. Like their predecessors Leopold and Loeb, whose crime formed the basis of Alfred Hitchcock's *Rope*, they thought it would be fun to see if they could outwit the authorities in a game of murder.

Mario was 26 years old and his friend was 27 when in August 1977 they decided to make their morbid fantasies a reality by setting a drug addict on fire and blaming it on a fictional neo-Nazi named 'Ludwig'. This was the first in a series of apparently random killings by the pair. Furlan and Abel targeted individuals whom they despised for reasons known only to themselves.

Both had everything that money could buy. Abel lived a life of luxury in the family home in the exclusive Verona suburb of Monte Ricco (Mountain of the Rich). His father was a former managing director of a West German insurance company. Furlan's father was a plastic surgeon whose income had bought a beautiful house in the suburbs of the city. But both young men were described as strange and isolated by their former classmates and fellow university students.

'LUDWIG' STRIKES AGAIN

The murder of the drug addict was followed by the fatal stabbing of a casino employee in Padua, the brutal beating and knifing of a homosexual writer in Venice, the axe murder of a prostitute and the killing of two priests in Vicenza. The priests were bludgeoned to death with hammers.

Another priest was later murdered when a nail was hammered into his head and a chisel was embedded in his brain. And in Verona a hitchhiker was burned to death while he slept, unable to free himself from his sleeping bag. Then five people died in an arson attack on a pornographic cinema in Milan.

The police were baffled. The killings were committed in different towns, the methods were

Abel (left) and Furlan invented an imaginary friend called Ludwig who they blamed for their crimes

dissimilar and there appeared to be nothing to link them other than the enigmatic letters that were left at each scene. Written in Italian, they were signed by the mysterious 'Ludwig'.

Each note was headed with a swastika and each bore a slogan such as 'We are the last Nazis'. But there was no forensic evidence with which to identify the writer and there was a considerable gap between incidents. Added to that, the random nature of the attacks made it impossible to predict where or when the killer, or killers, might strike next.

'FRAMED'

The police had their answer on the evening of 3 March 1984, when Abel and Furlan were caught attempting to set fire to furniture in a crowded disco near Mantua. When the friends' homes were searched, evidence was recovered linking Abel to the letters.

The pair's trial began on 1 December 1986 and it lasted until January. At its conclusion, each man was handed a 30-year sentence. Doubts as to their sanity saved them from a life sentence, but it was all academic because they were released soon afterwards for reasons which remain unknown. Critics of the Italian judiciary claim that their freedom was bought and paid for while others cite the judge's compassion for two young men who were clearly not in their right mind at the time of the murders. And there are some who say that the judges were uneasy at the idea of condemning men purely on the basis of circumstantial evidence. Only Furlan and Abel know the truth. They are currently under separate house arrest in the small villages of Mestrino and Casale di Scodosia in Padua, where they spend their days in idleness. However, they always welcome the chance to tell the story of how they were 'framed' for the crimes perpetrated by the elusive 'Ludwig'.

ALONG FOR THE RIDE –

JAMES MILLER AND CHRISTOPHER WORRELL

When James Miller recovered from the car crash that had killed Christopher Worrell and their companion Deborah Skuse in February 1977, he did not mourn his deceased friend. Miller's overwhelming feeling was one of relief. Now the killings would end and he would be free of Worrell's malevolent influence.

The three had been holidaying at Mount Gambier, one of Australia's favourite beauty spots, when Worrell complained that he was having another manic depressive episode. He then demanded that they drive back to Adelaide. Worrell was at the wheel when a tyre blew. Losing control, he sent the car into a roll that catapulted all three occupants into the road.

Miller was the only survivor. Quite quickly he decided that no good at all would come of telling the police that his friend had been a serial rapist and killer and he did not feel the need to confess to his own part in the crimes. The more he thought it through, the more he convinced himself that he had been an unwilling accomplice, a victim, the only one to survive.

But he did not keep his terrible secret for long.

On 25 April 1978 ramblers found a severed leg in scrub near Truro in South Australia. Most of the flesh had been eaten by wild dogs, or had fallen away, but a shoe and some painted toenails had survived. A search of the area recovered clothes and more human remains, which forensic experts were able to identify as belonging to 18-year-old Veronica Knight, who had been reported missing

> RAMBLERS FOUND A SEVERED LEG IN SCRUB... MOST OF THE FLESH HAD BEEN EATEN BY WILD DOGS... BUT A SHOE AND SOME PAINTED TOENAILS HAD SURVIVED

Dead men tell no tales: Worrell (below) died in a car crash, leaving the unreliable Miller to confess on his behalf

Blessing in disguise? Worrell rolled his car and died on the way back from Mount Gambier, the Australian beauty spot

from her home in Adelaide just before Christmas two years earlier. But there were no clues to her killer's identity.

Then a year later the remains of another teenage girl were found near the same site. These were identified as those of 16-year-old Sylvia Pittman, who had been reported missing at about the same time as Veronica Knight.

Now the police were certain that they were on to a serial killer, so they dug deeper into the missing persons' files and discovered that five more young women had disappeared in the area at around the same time.

The remains of two of these girls, Connie Iordanides and Vicki Howell, were soon located near the spot at which the first girl had been found, but neither of their corpses yielded clues that might lead to the arrest of their killer.

FUNERAL CONFESSION

It was only after these discoveries were reported in the newspapers in May 1979 that a former girlfriend of Christopher Worrell came forward and claimed the reward for naming him as their killer and Miller as his accomplice. She told police that at Worrell's funeral she and Miller had been discussing Worrell's mood swings. When she revealed that Worrell had been diagnosed with a blood clot on the brain, Miller thought it might explain his dead friend's violent outbursts and his compulsion to murder any girl who resisted him. He allegedly confided his thoughts to her.

'It was getting worse lately. It was happening more often. It was perhaps a good thing that Chris died.'

When she was asked why she had not reported this at the time, she said she thought Miller's confession might have been a symptom of his own mental instability. Also, if Worrell was dead there was little point in naming him as a serial rapist and murderer.

But the bereaved families needed to know who had murdered their daughters and so did the police. They grilled Miller, now a homeless middle-aged drifter. After initially denying all knowledge of the killings, he confessed to having taken part in seven murders, three of which the detectives had not been aware of. He admitted that he had been Worrell's lover in prison, where the latter had been serving time for armed robbery and rape, and that on their release they had lived together in what Miller described as a dominant and submissive relationship. But Worrell soon tired of his slave and was impatient to practise his deviant behaviour on women, preferably innocent, unwilling ones so he could get a thrill from their humiliation and distress. He was then in his early twenties and was considered handsome, so he had no trouble in picking up single girls from clubs, bus stops and shopping malls. Some might even have felt safer after seeing his friend Miller sitting in the passenger seat. In any case, serial killers were almost unheard of at that time in Australia.

Each time Worrell had the urge to rape and kill he would stop the car at a lonely spot and Miller would make himself scarce until he could be certain that the deed was done. On a couple of occasions he claimed to have returned to see Worrell tie a girl up and then strangle her. He also said that he once tried to save one of the girls, but Worrell fought him off. But if he thought his story would convince the police to discount him as an accomplice, he was deluding himself.

James Miller stood trial for all seven murders in March 1980 and was found guilty on six counts of aiding in a criminal conspiracy. He was sentenced to six terms of life imprisonment. His lawyer argued that his client had not taken part in the actual killings and that he had no idea his former lover would kill the girls they had picked up, but the judge made it clear in his summing up that Miller must have known the likely outcome and that walking away from the murder did not absolve him of responsibility. The fact remained he had been present when each girl was enticed into the car and he had assisted in the disposal of the bodies.

Miller was due for parole in 2014, but he died from cancer on 21 October 2008. He was 68 years old.

EACH TIME WORRELL HAD THE URGE TO RAPE AND KILL, HE WOULD STOP THE CAR AND MILLER WOULD MAKE HIMSELF SCARCE UNTIL THE DEED WAS DONE

DEATH DOWN UNDER –

DAVID AND
CATHERINE BIRNIE

It was like a scene from a trashy stalk 'n' slash horror movie, except that in this instance the victim was truly in fear of her life and her attackers were for real. The location was Willagee, a suburb of Perth, Australia and the date was 10 November 1986. Seventeen-year-old Kate Moir ran naked and screaming into a grocery store on Moorhouse Street, where she blurted out the incredible story of how she had been held at knifepoint by a homicidal couple who had chained her to a bed and repeatedly raped her. It was only by chance she had managed to escape through a window when no one was around – the man was away and the woman had neglected to secure her when she went to answer the front door.

The police were summoned and the hysterical girl calmed down sufficiently to accompany them to the house where the owner, Catherine Birnie, admitted that she knew the girl. However, she refused to say anything more until her husband returned. David Birnie was arrested at his workplace and brought home in handcuffs to be questioned. The Birnies then concocted a story that cast the distraught girl as a willing sex partner who had smoked too much cannabis and was now confused about events.

The police were sceptical and so were inclined

to believe the victim, but they knew that they could not charge the couple without proof. There would have to be a confession or forensic evidence which proved that the girl had been forcibly abducted, imprisoned in their home and then raped. Their only hope was to wear the Birnies down by subjecting them to a prolonged and intense interrogation. By nightfall the couple had still not cracked, so with nothing to lose Detective Sergeant Vince Katich played a wild card.

'It's getting dark. Best we take the shovel and dig them up,' he said to David Birnie.

To his amazement Birnie nodded.

'Okay,' he said. 'There are four of them.'

David Birnie exhibited a morbid pride in taking the detectives to the graves, where he relived the torment he had inflicted on each of the four young women who had been at his mercy. It was clear to the police that they were dealing with a deranged individual. They were more likely to draw out a detailed confession if they appealed to his vanity.

NEIGHBOURS FROM HELL

David John Birnie was born on 16 February 1951, to a family that locals referred to as the 'neighbours from hell'. It was said the parents were alcoholics who practised incest and that David Birnie had

David Birnie took a morbid pride in the torment he had inflicted; Catherine abandoned seven children for his company

Fatal collision: Birnie was working in a car wrecking yard when Mary Neilson appeared in search of tyres

been a teenage apprentice jockey who had mutilated the horses and raped an old woman.

Birnie had been in and out of jail for minor offences all through his teens and his twenties, but he had managed to marry and father a child before he left his wife for Catherine Margaret Birnie (who was also born in 1951). She had been raised by her maternal grandparents after her mother had died, but at the age of ten her father decided that he wanted her back. He fought and won a custody battle which ensured that she lived with him until the age of 14, when she took up with David Birnie. Her father disapproved of the relationship, which only intensified her determination to be with Birnie. But their relationship led to her conviction for petty crimes, for which she was sent to prison. Once she was free of his malevolent influence she reformed herself and on her release she took a job as a housekeeper for a respectable family, the McLaughlins. She eventually married their

son, David, on her 21st birthday and the couple had seven children before Birnie reappeared. But then he persuaded her to leave her husband and children to live with him.

The couple moved to a modest bungalow on Moorhouse Street in Willagee and there they lived as husband and wife, although they did not marry. Catherine merely changed her name by deed poll in order to demonstrate her devotion to her man. However, their shared sexual fantasies of rape and murder were not enough for them. By late 1986 they burned with a desire to live them out for real.

FANTASY BECOMES REALITY

The opportunity to satisfy their craving occurred on 6 October, when 22-year-old student Mary Neilson drove into the car wrecking yard where Birnie worked. She asked him if she could buy some tyres and Birnie told her that he had a set at home that he could sell her for a good price. He arranged to see her there after work. When Mary arrived that evening Birnie whipped out a knife and forced her into the bedroom, where she was bound and gagged. There he raped her repeatedly while Catherine watched. She was egging him on like some demented cheerleader. When he had satiated his lust and was tiring of his new slave, they drove Mary to Gleneagles National Park in the dead of night, where Birnie assaulted her again. Then he strangled her with a cord and stabbed her through the heart. The pair of them dumped her body in a shallow grave and then returned home to gloat about it.

Two weeks later they were impatient to repeat the experience so they kidnapped 15-year-old Susannah Candy as she walked home along Stirling Highway in Claremont. Back at the bungalow the Birnies held a knife to her throat and threatened to kill her unless she wrote to her family. Her message was that she had gone to Queensland with friends and would never return. Then she too was gagged, chained to the bed and repeatedly raped. But when David Birnie tried to strangle her with a cord she fought back and they had to sedate her with sleeping pills. Then Catherine throttled her while she lay unconscious. Susannah was buried later that night in the State Forest.

On 1 November they stalked their third victim, 31-year-old Noelene Patterson, who had run out of petrol on the Canning Highway. She was subjected to the same ordeal as the others, but instead of killing her that night David Birnie kept her as his sex slave for three days while he and Catherine argued over what to do with her. He wanted to keep her, but Catherine demanded that he finish her off before he became too attached to her. Either that

or Catherine would kill herself in a jealous rage. He soon relented. After force-feeding the terrified girl with sleeping pills he then strangled her. She was buried with the other bodies while Catherine spat abuse and threw sand in her face.

Their final victim, apart from the escapee Kate Moir, was 21-year-old Denise Brown. On 5 November they snatched her at a bus stop on Stirling Highway and drove her to the bungalow in Moorhouse Street, where she was bound and raped. That night they took her to the Wanneroo pine plantation where she was stabbed while Birnie raped her. Then they threw her into a shallow grave, but she was not dead. When she tried to get up Birnie struck her twice on the head with an axe and then shovelled more dirt over her.

This was the core of David Birnie's confession and he stuck to it, pleading guilty at his trial to all four counts of murder and one count each of abduction and rape. His co-defendant shared his sentence of four consecutive terms of life imprisonment, which required them to serve 20 years before being eligible for parole.

During their incarceration the couple sent a total of more than 2,500 letters to each other, none of which expressed remorse or regret other than for the fact that they had been caught.

David Birnie committed suicide in his cell in 2005, while awaiting trial for the rape of another inmate. There were no mourners at his internment. Catherine Birnie remains in Bandyup Women's Prison, with no hope of parole. Western Australian attorney-general Christian Porter revoked her right to apply for release in March 2009. Her file bears the stamp, 'never to be released'. To date no one has contested the decision.

THE MONSTERS OF MONTMARTRE –
THIERRY PAULIN AND JEAN-THIERRY MATHURIN

Some individuals never come to terms with their sexual identity and prefer to blame others for the confusion and guilt that it brings them. Guyana-born transvestite Thierry Paulin blamed his grandmother for the neurosis that drove him to murder 21 elderly women in the Parisian district of Montmartre between 1984 and 1987. His lover, Jean-Thierry Mathurin, from Martinique, played an active part in the torture of nine of the victims to please his partner and to earn a share of the cocaine with which they celebrated each slaying.

The victims were all found bound, gagged and beaten in their homes before being strangled, suffocated or smothered. One had been force-fed caustic soda and another had been stabbed 60 times. This told the police that they were hunting a psychotic individual who was re-enacting the same revenge scenario over and over again. The victims' homes were then ransacked in a search for

Thierry Paulin blamed his grandmother for the neurosis that drove him to murder 21 elderly women in the district of Montmartre

Paulin (above and in drag) died before he could be sentenced; his accomplice Mathurin got life, but was freed in 2009

cash and jewellery, which indicated that the killer must have had an accomplice – it was unlikely that someone in a violent rage would have been capable of such rational behaviour. The torture of the victims was his primary motive.

But Paulin and Mathurin had already left the city when the Paris police rounded up every sex offender they could find. They were living the high life in Toulouse, where they snorted coke and partied in the most exclusive gay clubs in town. Then like all thieves they fell out, leaving Paulin to return alone to the capital where he was soon arrested for a violent assault on a drug dealer. He was released from prison in 1987, before he had served his full 16-month sentence, when

he resumed his killing spree. But one elderly victim lived long enough to give the police a good description. She told them her attacker was a black man with dyed platinum blond hair and large earrings. When Paulin was arrested on 1 December he immediately broke down and confessed, but he was not going to go down without taking his old partner and lover with him. The trial gave him the attention and recognition he craved. He appeared in court dressed like a garish imitation of Norma Desmond, the deranged silent movie queen in the film *Sunset Boulevard*. But his days in the spotlight were numbered. He died of AIDS on 16 April 1989, before his guilt could be proven beyond doubt.

SINS OF THE FATHER –
AGNES AND ANDRAS PANDY

Mousey, middle-aged Agnes Pandy stared blankly from behind her prescription spectacles at the detective who had just entered the interview room at Brussels police headquarters. As he sat down and pulled out a pen to make his preliminary notes, he must have wondered what information the dowdy librarian might have that could be of use to him. When she spoke it was in a voice as expressionless as her face: 'I am my father's sex slave.'

GRAPHIC DETAIL

She then described in graphic detail the bullying and abuse she claimed she had been subjected to from the age of 13. But that was not all. That spring afternoon in 1992 she also accused her father of murdering her stepmother Edit Fintor and her stepsister Andrea four years earlier. Agnes and her older brother had been sent away to the coast and when they returned her father had a message for them. 'Don't look for them. They're not coming back.'

FRUSTRATED SPINSTER

The detective was not inclined to believe her incredible story. For one thing her father was a respectable Protestant pastor in Molenbeek,

an impoverished district in the Belgian capital. And besides, the 'victim' was thought to be alive and well and living in Eastern Europe. In a lengthy interview later that day Pastor Pandy vigorously dismissed his daughter's accusations as the fantasies of a frustrated spinster who had been pathologically jealous of her stepmother. He suggested that the impressionable Agnes had been brainwashed by a religious sect who implanted false memories in their members to alienate them from their families. As for the lurid accusations of murder, Pandy was able to produce

WHEN THE DOWDY LIBRARIAN SPOKE IT WAS IN A VOICE AS EXPRESSIONLESS AS HER FACE: 'I AM MY FATHER'S SEX SLAVE'

Family affair: Agnes claimed that incest had led her father to murder, but no one believed what she was saying to them

letters purporting to be from his estranged second wife, which appeared to substantiate his story that she had returned to Hungary with her daughter, some years earlier. Subsequent enquiries revealed that he had registered her as 'missing' at the time of her disappearance in 1987. Fortunately for him the investigating officer was traced and when questioned he recalled how distraught Pandy had seemed at the time. If the pastor had been putting on an act, it had been a very convincing performance.

THE DUTROUX FACTOR

The police were inclined to dismiss the abuse as a story told by a neurotic girl desperate for attention, so the report was stamped 'case closed', filed away and forgotten. Forgotten, that is, until 1997 when the file was reopened in response to the public outcry surrounding an unrelated case, that of child killer Marc Dutroux. It had been rumoured that prominent members of the Belgian establishment might have conspired to cover up Dutroux's crimes in order to divert attention from

*Waste disposal: Agnes used a kitchen knife to take out the organs of victims, while her father cut up the remains

their alleged involvement in a paedophile ring. So in a desperate effort to refute the rumours and restore public confidence in the judicial system the Belgian authorities ordered all cold case files to be reopened and all unproven accusations over the past decade to be re-examined. It was an instinctive response to quieten public anger and it was not expected to produce any results. But in such trying times even the word of a pastor could be questioned.

Agnes was recalled to police headquarters, where she was closely questioned. In the wake of the Dutroux scandal she had been making accusations in the Belgian press, which had forced the authorities to look more closely at her original statement.

'I am ashamed that my father might turn out to be one of the worst serial killers in history,' she had told a reporter.

Such serious allegations demanded thorough and immediate investigation.

DISSOLVING THE BODIES

This time she was interviewed by senior prosecutor François Monsieur who took her story more seriously. Sensing that she was finally being listened to, Agnes opened up and spoke for a total of seven hours over a two-day period. Her story shocked even the hardened prosecutor, who struggled to maintain an appearance of professional detachment while she recalled the clinical means by which she and her father had butchered six members of their own family and disposed of the remains. Between 1986 and 1992 they had killed Ilona Sores, Edit Fintor and her daughters Tunde and Andrea as well as Agnes' two younger brothers, Zoltan and Daniel.

'It was my task to take out the organs while he [Pandy] was cutting up the remains,' she confessed as if describing a routine household chore. 'I just used a kitchen knife... you have to exercise strength. It's not that easy.'

She had eviscerated one of her own stepsisters while her father had chopped up the corpse with an axe. When asked to describe how she had felt the only word she could summon was 'cold'. Agnes claimed that they had dismembered the victims and then dumped bags of bloody flesh at the local abattoir, hoping that no one would notice the difference between human remains and horsemeat. But there was too much evidence to dispose of in that way and besides, the heads and the limbs would have to be destroyed. These were dropped into a bath of household cleaning fluid and chemically dissolved until nothing identifiable remained but human soup, which could be flushed down the drain.

When the case came to court, prosecutors feared that the jury might look at the two unprepossessing individuals in the dock and find it impossible to believe that they could have dismembered and disposed of so many corpses.

And so they devised a demonstration in which forensic scientists dissolved body parts in a vat of the household cleaning fluid. The remains had been harvested from a man who had died of natural causes and had donated his body to science. As Agnes had predicted the flesh simply melted from the bones. The experiment was filmed and the footage was shown in court. Pandy watched the video impassively. Agnes turned away.

Pandy was sentenced to life imprisonment on six counts of murder. Agnes got 21 years.

Andras Pandy was a Belgian Protestant pastor of Hungarian origin – the press dubbed him 'Father Bluebeard'

THE RAGE OF CALIBAN –

JOHN BROWN AND SAMUEL COETZEE

South Africa has seen more than its fair share of bloodshed in its history, but the country that only comparatively recently shook off the shackles of apartheid and reinvented itself as the 'rainbow nation' now has to accept that no country can be immune to the sordid reality that is murder.

Between 1993 and 1995 the country's newspaper headlines were dominated not by politics but by a series of violent murders and the frantic hunt for the perpetrators.

The first body was discovered on 30 August 1993, on a gravel road near Pretoria. On 3 November 1993 two more corpses were found near the town of Heidelberg – those of an unidentified 15-year-old boy and a 30-year-old man. Both had suffered bullet and stab wounds and both had ligature marks around the throat. Such injuries are indicative of 'overkill' – wounds which must have been inflicted by a person in a rage because they were far beyond what would have been needed to kill a person. No attempt had been made to cover the face in either case so the police were confident that the killer had no personal relationship with his victim before the fatal date.

STRANGLED AND MUTILATED

A fourth victim, who had been strangled and mutilated, was found at Krugersdorp on 1 September 1995. His genitals had been cut off, suggesting that the killer was likely to be either a woman or a homosexual male. But because the

> TWO MORE CORPSES WERE FOUND... BOTH HAD SUFFERED BULLET AND STAB WOUNDS AND BOTH HAD LIGATURE MARKS AROUND THE THROAT

Alter egos: 'serial killer' Samuel Coetzee (above and 'dragged-up' to go clubbing). He was also known as 'Kim'

other victims were all too strongly built to have been subdued by a female, detectives worked on the assumption that the murderer was a homosexual male.

Gay clubs throughout the region were visited and the owners and customers were shown photographs of the victims. Several witnesses remembered seeing the dead men in the company of a known cross-dresser called 'Kim'. Inquiries revealed that his real name was Samuel Coetzee, then aged 26. But before he could be questioned a fifth body took detectives to a house in Constantia Court, Edenvale. Inquiries confirmed that this victim had also been seen leaving a night club with

Coetzee. When he was arrested Coetzee blamed his lover John Brown for the killings and claimed that he had only disposed of the bodies.

When 32-year-old Brown was brought in he attempted to put the blame on Coetzee. His only interest had been to rob the men. It was Coetzee, he said, who murdered them in a frenzied attack.

Before the truth could be drawn out of them Coetzee took an overdose of pills in his cell and died, leaving a suicide note saying he no longer wanted to go on living. In 1997, Brown was sentenced to life imprisonment and the following day the newspapers returned to the more immediate concerns of politics, scandal and sport.

CHAPTER 6

KILLING WITHOUT CONSCIENCE

Modern life is murder. At the turn of the 21st century when we can boast the invention of the internet, laser surgery and space travel, it is difficult to appreciate that, as a species, we are still barely out of the jungle in terms of evolution. For some psychologically unsound individuals, the pressures of conforming in a world obsessed with status and achievement can be unsettling. Some take drastic action to be noticed — even though the attention they get will inevitably be negative in the extreme.

THE HILLSIDE STRANGLER CASE –

KENNETH BIANCHI AND ANGELO BUONO

What do you say to the distraught parents of a young murder victim? This was the dilemma faced by Los Angeles homicide detective Bob Grogan when the parents of 20-year-old honours student Kristina Weckler came to identify their daughter's body at the county morgue in November 1977. Grogan had a teenage daughter of his own so he could imagine how the Wecklers must be feeling.

Earlier that day he had visited Kristina's apartment in Glendale, where he looked at her belongings and leafed through her diary for clues as to the identity of her killer. But he found nothing, only the evidence of a life cruelly cut short, of hopes unfulfilled. It had made him angry. He could cope with the killings of hookers and junkies downtown – at least they knew the risks – but this was a 'nice girl', the daughter of middle-class parents, and she was not the first to die that year.

There had been three other female victims before Kristina: Yolanda Washington, Judy Miller and Lissa Kastin. They had all been strangled and their naked bodies had been left on the hillsides northeast of Los Angeles. And there would be more, no doubt about it, until the killers were caught.

The suspicion that there might be more than one person involved came from the fact that there were no drag marks at the site in Highland Park and the foliage had not been crushed. Two men must have carried the body and then set it down on the grass.

Grogan promised Mr and Mrs Weckler that he would bring their daughter's murderers to justice. It was all he could do. They nodded but did not take it in. They had their daughter's belongings to pack and her funeral to arrange once the coroner had agreed to release the body. If they had registered his assurance, they did not respond. But he meant what he said and as he left the apartment that

> THERE HAD BEEN THREE OTHER VICTIMS BEFORE KRISTINA – THEY HAD ALL BEEN STRANGLED AND THEIR NAKED BODIES LEFT ON HILLSIDES

Killing cousins: Angelo Buono (above) and Kenneth Bianchi were very different characters with very similar interests

Victims of 'the Hillside Strangler' were dumped in the hills above LA

morning he silently vowed to keep his word.

From the dark bands around her neck, wrists and ankles it was clear that Kristina had been tied down and throttled. There were no track marks on her arms so she was not an addict, but there was bruising on her breasts and there were needle marks, betraying the fact that she had been tortured. Blood could be seen around the rectum, which indicated that sodomy had taken place, but tests made on semen found at the scene proved inconclusive. The primary perpetrator must be a non-secretor, someone whose blood group and DNA cannot be determined from their bodily fluids. An investigator's nightmare.

If Grogan had wanted a day to think things through he was not going to get it. That same afternoon his partner, Detective Dudley Varney, was summoned to the scene of a double murder just a mile away in Elysian Park. The bodies of two young girls had been found on a rubbish heap in an advanced state of decomposition. The ants were already at work. Again there was no disturbance of the ground, supporting the theory that there were two perpetrators. This was confirmed by several witnesses, who had seen the schoolgirls talking to a man sitting in the passenger seat of a two-tone sedan. The victims were later identified as 12-year-old Dolores Cepeda and 14-year-old Sonja Johnson.

The seventh victim was found on 23 November, near the Golden State Freeway. Jane King was 28 years old. She had been dead for a fortnight.

SEARCHING FOR A LEAD

The investigation into what the press were now calling the Hillside Strangler (it was supposed that only one killer was involved) was made a priority. A 30-man unit from the Los Angeles Police Department (LAPD), Glendale Police Department and the sheriff's office pooled their resources and shared the few leads that they had. But they had nothing of significance to go on – certainly not enough to prevent the killers from committing an eighth murder.

SENSIBLE GIRL

Eighteen-year-old student Lauren Wagner lived at home with her parents in the San Fernando Valley. When she did not come home on the night of 28 November her mother and father assumed that she would be in later. Lauren was a sensible girl and they could trust her. But when she had not returned by the next morning her father became anxious. His anxiety gave way to panic when he looked out and saw his daughter's car parked across the street with the driver's door wide open. He ran to the neighbouring houses and asked if anyone had seen her. Beulah Stofer had seen something. Lauren's car had been parked outside her house and a noisy argument had brought Beulah to the window. Looking out she had seen a young woman struggling with two men.

'You won't get away with it!' she had heard the girl shout.

Then the girl was hauled inside the men's vehicle and driven away. But the old woman told herself that it was probably a domestic squabble. It was only when she received a threatening telephone call the next day and saw Lauren's car in the daylight that she realized that it had been her neighbour's daughter. All she could remember when questioned about the incident was that

there had been two men. One was tall with a pockmarked face and the other was older, shorter and of Latin appearance, with bushy hair. She had not thought to note down their number plate but she remembered that their car was dark with a white top.

That afternoon Detective Sergeant Grogan had to make out another crime scene report. Lauren Wagner's naked body had been found on a hillside at Mount Washington in Glendale. Her body bore the same ligature marks and punctures as the previous victim's, as well as burn patches on the palms of the hands.

TAUNTING THE POLICE

Victims nine and ten were found in mid-December 1977 and February 1978, but neither body offered any more clues. The first corpse belonged to escort agency 'model' Kimberly Martin, who was dumped

> LAUREN WAGNER'S BODY BORE THE SAME LIGATURE MARKS AS THE PREVIOUS VICTIM'S, AS WELL AS BURN PATCHES ON THE HANDS

Needle in a haystack: police didn't have much to go on in tracking down a single vehicle among all the cars in LA

in Echo Park, and the second to Cindy Hudspeth, a clerk. She had been murdered on her way to her evening job at a local college. Cindy's corpse had been locked in the boot of her car which had then been pushed off the road and down a steep embankment at Angeles Crest.

It was as if the killers were taunting the police by dropping bodies almost on their doorstep. By this time Bob Grogan had been partnered with Detective Frank Salerno of the sheriff's department, but these two highly experienced officers could not get their teeth into a case that continually led to a dead end. Even the profilers could not offer more than a standard description of a single white male in his late twenties or early thirties, who was of average intelligence and was now cold and manipulative as a result of a brutal upbringing.

On reading the report Grogan sighed. 'All we got to do now is find a white male who hates his mother.' Someone had the bright idea of bringing in a psychic, but this added little to the profile other than the suggestion that they should be looking for two Italian brothers in their thirties.

It was not that far off the mark as it turned out, but at the time it did not provide a lead the investigators could follow.

And then the curtain rose on the second act.

THE 'FRIENDLY' SECURITY GUARD

Two university students, Karen Mandic and Diane Wilder, were reported missing in Bellingham, Washington on 12 January 1979. Karen's boss told detectives that she had told him about a part-time house-sitting job she had taken in the exclusive suburb of Bayside. It was such an unusual opportunity that Karen had told her boss quite a bit about the circumstances that led to the offer, including the name of the security guard and the firm he worked for. When questioned, the man denied knowing either of the girls and claimed that he had been at a meeting on the evening they had disappeared. But his story did not check out.

At that stage Bellingham's chief of police, Terry Mangan, had a hunch so he decided to take charge of the investigation himself. He went to the apartment that Karen and Diane had shared, where he found the address of the house in Bayside that the girls had agreed to look after. When the security firm searched their files they confirmed that the guard had been assigned to watch the property, but had taken a company truck for repair on the night in question. However, the workshop had no record of the truck being serviced on that date.

A wet footprint was then found in the house but there was no sign of the girls, so Mangan ordered his men to make discreet inquiries in the neighbourhood. He suspected a kidnapping and did not want to panic the abductors into killing the girls in order to cover their tracks.

Finally, a neighbour informed the police that a security guard had asked her to keep a watch on the house, but on the night the girls disappeared he told her to keep away. The alarm system was faulty, he said, and he did not want her to trigger it accidentally.

Now was the time to issue a description of the girls and their car to the media in the hope that someone might have seen them that night. The police were in luck. Someone had seen the girls' car, which had been abandoned in a remote area. Their bodies were found inside. They had been strangled and beaten. Chief Mangan immediately ordered that the security guard be brought in for questioning. His name was Kenneth Bianchi.

UNUSUAL SUSPECT

Bianchi was a most unusual suspect. An amiable handsome man with an apparently friendly disposition, he was well liked by his employer and was considered a real gentleman by his girlfriend, Kelli Boyd, who was the mother of their young son. But when the police delved into his background they came across a totally different person. He was the son of a hooker who had given him up for adoption at birth.

Perhaps as a result, the boy became overly dependent on his foster mother. In adulthood he remained immature and irresponsible and he was also a practised, pathological liar, who thought nothing of gaining Kelli's sympathy by telling her that he was terminally ill.

Bianchi seemed like the archetypal 'good guy', an amiable handsome man with an apparently friendly disposition

He was also fastidious about the way his women dressed and he was liable to erupt into a childish tantrum if a girlfriend disobeyed his explicit instructions. His strict Catholic upbringing had conditioned him to expect every woman he went with to act in a prim and proper fashion and when they expressed a mind of their own he would become furious.

If they left him, he felt betrayed. He desired women but despised them for making him feel that way. It was the classic mindset for a serial rapist and a killer of women.

THE WOULD-BE COP

Bianchi longed to enrol in the police force, but he failed to pass the entrance exams and so he had taken to working as a security guard as the next best thing. It gave him the sense of authority and self-respect he craved and it also gave him an opportunity to steal any items that caught his eye. When the Bellingham police searched his apartment they found an Aladdin's cave of loot, which enabled them to hold him while forensics ran tests on fibres and hairs found on the two dead girls and in the house on Bayside. Pubic hairs from the girls were found inside the vacant house and Bianchi freely admitted that he was the only person who had access to the property, other than the neighbour he had told about the 'faulty alarm' on the night the girls went missing. Among the articles of jewellery they recovered were two items belonging to victims Kimberly Martin and Yolanda Washington. They had him nailed. All they needed now was a confession and the name of his partner. But Bianchi was so wrapped up in his own fantasy world that it was impossible to know when he was being candid and when he was being deceitful.

FANTASY WORLD

When he was not strutting around in his uniform he could not resist the urge to pose as a psychologist and counsellor, so he had set himself up in business with a set of fake qualifications and a hired office. Fortunately, no one trusted him with their secrets so he gave it in soon afterwards.

But the ambition to be a policeman did not recede so easily. While the hunt for the Hillside Strangler was at its height Bianchi talked the LAPD into allowing him to ride along with the patrolmen as part of a community relations programme. But all he did that night was drone on about the killings. It should have sounded alarm bells with the officers, but they were presumably just glad to get rid of him at the end of their shift.

Bianchi had been living in Los Angeles at the time of the 1977 murders and the police had interviewed him about one of the killings in his apartment block.

But he made such a convincing witness that he was not questioned a second time. The reason that the killings stopped in 1978 and then started up again in Bellingham in 1979 was that Kelli moved there after they separated and Bianchi followed, hoping for a reconciliation.

Chief Mangan was aware of Bianchi's history so he thought it was probably worth contacting the LAPD to check on his movements at the time of the Glendale killings.

Detective Frank Salerno took the call and was able to confirm that Bianchi had been living in the same street as Cindy Hudspeth and Kristina Weckler at the time of their murders. He had then moved to the apartment where Kimberly Martin had gone to meet a client before she vanished.

The final piece of the puzzle fell into place after the Los Angeles police circulated a photograph of Bianchi to the media, with a request for information. Among the many responses was a call from a lawyer, David Wood, who claimed to have saved a girl from a prostitution ring run by Bianchi and his cousin, Angelo Buono.

BUONO WAS CRUDE, HOSTILE AND CLEARLY UNTRUSTWORTHY — A REAL THUG. HE HAD SOMETHING TO HIDE AND IT WAS A BIG UGLY SECRET

THE 'ITALIAN STALLION'

Detective Grogan lost no time in tracking down Angelo so that he could grill him on his movements on the critical dates. He was accompanied on the drive down by Salerno's partner Pete Finnigan. They had a feeling that Buono was the right man the moment they met him. He was crude, hostile and clearly untrustworthy – a real thug. He was also antagonistic from the outset, on the defensive as soon as the cops mentioned that they were following up a lead on Becky Spears and Sabra Hannan, two of the girls from his prostitution ring. He had something to hide and it was a big ugly secret. The more they probed him for details and dates, the more aggressive and uneasy he became. He bared his crooked teeth in barely disguised contempt and ran his dirty fingers through his dyed black hair as he glared from one cop to the other and back again.

This was the self-titled 'Italian Stallion' who had called his mother a whore to her face and had abused his numerous lovers. He had been married several times, but he made no secret of his loathing for women, who found him primitively attractive until he had beaten them black and blue. Even as a teenager he had bragged of raping and sodomizing girls in the neighbourhood and he was a known admirer of serial rapist Caryl Chessman, who had passed himself off as a policeman to lure prostitutes into his car. Former girlfriends and wives had accused him of sexually abusing his own children and of threatening anyone who dared to leave him. And yet underage girls had been attracted by his cocksure arrogance and animal magnetism. It was one of the things that attracted his cousin Kenneth Bianchi to him in the autumn of 1975. Kenneth hoped he could pull the girls that hung around Angelo and maybe learn a few tricks from the big bad wolf. The first scam he learnt was how to get free sex from a hooker by flashing a fake police badge when the deed was done. The girls were out of the car and down the street before the cousins had stopped grinning.

'You can't let a c**t get the upper hand,' he told Bianchi. 'Put them in their place.'

PROSTITUTION RING

It was not long before they had the idea to work their own prostitution ring by recruiting teenage runaways and threatening them with violence if they objected or withheld their earnings. But then one of the girls met lawyer David Wood, who helped her to leave the city. Soon afterwards the second girl escaped. Angelo was not going to let Wood get away with derailing his gravy train, but Wood knew how to deal with thugs like Angelo. He sent one of his heavies round – a former client – who let the would-be pimp know that it would be in his best interests to let the girl go. Write her off as damaged goods, so to speak.

But Angelo was not a man to be pushed around or put off when he could smell easy money. So he roped his cousin into his next scheme, which was abducting a girl off the street and setting her up as their private prostitute. But first they had to invest in a list of 'Johns' who were regular customers of the girls that plied their trade on Sunset Boulevard. When the list turned out to be a fake they swore they would skin the hooker alive who sold it to them, but they could not find her so they abducted and killed her friend, Yolanda Washington, instead. And that is how the Hillside Stranglers started.

A KILLER'S ALTER EGO

Once in custody Kenneth Bianchi was informed that the case against him was rock solid and that if he did not co-operate he would be facing the death penalty. Cornered, Bianchi resorted to an old trick from his childhood. He rolled his eyes up inside his head and pretended that he could remember nothing. When that did not get him the sympathy he was seeking, he faked a multiple personality disorder. He had been watching television in his cell when a movie on the subject had given him the idea. By the time an expert had been dispatched to test him, Bianchi had rehearsed his routine. It was a good enough performance to convince Dr John G. Watkins, but Detective Salerno had spotted the critical slips in Bianchi's story. On several occasions he referred to his homicidal alter ego, Steve Walker, in the third person instead of the first as if telling a story that had happened to someone else. If the disorder had been genuine he would have used 'I' and not 'he'.

Detective Grogan greeted the news with his customary wry humour. He told Salerno that he would ask the judge to set Bianchi free but send 'Steve Walker' to Death Row. That would give him something to work on. The detectives grew even more despondent when the court-appointed psychiatrist Dr Ralph B. Allison confirmed the diagnosis. Bianchi was not faking, he said. Then the prosecution brought in their own expert, Dr Martin T. Orne, who immediately contradicted his two colleagues. Dr Orne gave Bianchi a number of rigorous tests designed to rule out anyone who was shamming. He concluded that the subject was indeed faking.

But Dr Orne was not going to engage in a credibility contest with his colleagues. He knew that the court would weigh his conclusions against the two experts who disagreed with him and would most likely favour them, so he threw a wild card into the game. As he was packing away his papers he told Bianchi that it was very rare to find a subject who had only one personality squatting in his head. It was more common to find subjects tormented by three or more.

Bianchi took the bait just as Dr Orne had hoped. He created a second uninvited guest, who would share the blame for the killings with the fictional 'Steve'. Dr Orne's scepticism was shared by another independent expert, Dr Saul Faerstein, who had been called in by the prosecution to give a second opinion. With the odds now even, Bianchi was prepared to drop his act and listen to a one-time offer from the district attorney.

If he admitted his part in the Bellingham and

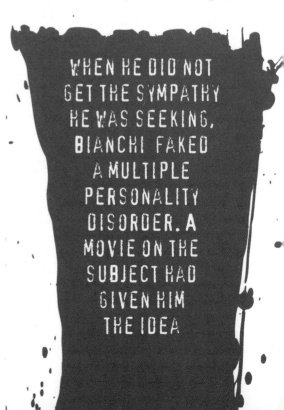

WHEN HE DID NOT GET THE SYMPATHY HE WAS SEEKING, BIANCHI FAKED A MULTIPLE PERSONALITY DISORDER. A MOVIE ON THE SUBJECT HAD GIVEN HIM THE IDEA

Buono was an admirer of the serial rapist Caryl Chessman who passed himself off as a policeman to lure prostitutes into his car

Glendale murders and was prepared to testify against Angelo Buono he would get life, with the chance of parole at some unspecified future date. The death penalty would be off the table. It was an offer he could not afford to refuse.

THE COUSINS STAND TRIAL

Bianchi's confession was supported by photographic line-up identifications made by two eyewitnesses (Beulah Stofer the elderly neighbour who had witnessed Lauren Wagner's abduction and Markust Camden, who had seen the kidnapping of Judy Miller). In addition there was compelling forensic evidence. Material found on the bodies of Judy Miller and Lauren Wagner was peculiar to Angelo's home and upholstery workshop, a place where he worked alone. And the rabbit hairs found on Lauren's corpse matched the pets that Angelo kept. Together this was enough to secure an arrest warrant for cousin Angelo.

Detectives are trained to be impartial and objective so that the evidence decides the guilt or innocence of a suspect. It is imperative that they are non-judgmental when interviewing someone accused of a particularly vile crime. If they betray a hint of revulsion, they risk the suspect clamming up. But on 22 October 1979 Detective Sergeant Bob Grogan could not mask the deep satisfaction he felt when he handcuffed Angelo Buono and read him his rights. Grogan would readily admit that it would take a far more forgiving man than he was to have treated the murderer of Kristina Weckler and at least nine other women with impartiality (Buono was finally convicted of killing eight people).

Like so many criminals, Angelo was stupid beyond belief. After the well-publicized arrest of his cousin he had not thought to dispose of his wallet, which betrayed the imprint of the fake police badge with which he had conned the prostitutes. But just when the investigation team was congratulating itself on a job well done, Kenneth Bianchi pulled another infuriating stunt.

He got cold feet at the thought of testifying against his cousin, which would have made him an informer, so he retracted his confession and named another man. It was someone he had obviously dreamt up in an effort to sidetrack the police and cast doubts on his own culpability.

Bianchi played the confused, mentally unstable witness to the best of his ability when he was called to the stand on 6 July 1981, but the judge was having none of it. His contempt for the witness was only several degrees higher than his disdain for the district attorney, who had moved to have the case dismissed for fear his conviction record would be spoiled by an acquittal.

Judge George ruled that dismissal would not be

> KENNETH BIANCHI PULLED ANOTHER INFURIATING STUNT. HE GOT COLD FEET AT THE THOUGHT OF TESTIFYING AGAINST BUONO

Police dragnet: Roger Boren, deputy Attorney General of California, in front of gory pictures of the 'Hillside Strangler' victims

'in the furtherance of justice... nor is it the function of the court automatically to rubber-stamp the prosecutor's decision to abandon the People's case.'

District Attorney Kelly had been warned. The charges against Angelo must be made and answered before a jury. Politics had no place in the court room. Smarting from his public reprimand the district attorney withdrew, forcing the attorney general to appoint four special prosecutors to consider the strength of the case against Buono. Their decision was unanimous. Buono must answer the charges.

After numerous delaying tactics the case finally came to court in November 1981, but Bianchi was still playing the prima donna. Then the judge reminded Bianchi that he was within his rights to send him to a more Spartan institution if he violated the conditions of his plea bargain by changing his story. From then on he played ball. But the case did not hinge on Bianchi, even if he believed it did. During the two-year trial more than 250 witnesses placed Buono at the scene of the crimes and testified to his sadistic impulses.

On 31 October 1983 the foreman of the jury handed the clerk of the court the jury's first verdict. It related to the murder of Lauren Wagner. There could be no doubt. It was guilty. There followed

The judge reminded Bianchi that if he refused to co-operate he would be sent to a much tougher jail. Bianchi co-operated

eight more guilty verdicts and only one not guilty. The murder of Yolanda Washington could not be proved.

Buono had the nerve to protest that his rights had been violated, but no one was listening. For reasons known only to itself the jury voted to spare Buono from the death penalty, which angered Judge Ronald George, who reminded them of the seriousness of the charges.

'Angelo Buono and Kenneth Bianchi subjected various of their murder victims to the administration of lethal gas, electrocution, strangulation by rope, and lethal hypodermic injection. Yet the two defendants are destined to spend their lives in prison, housed, fed and clothed at taxpayer expense, better cared for than some of the destitute law-abiding members of our community.'

Buono spent the first part of his sentence in Folsom Prison, where he refused to come out of his cell in case other inmates imposed their own brand of justice on the woman beater. He died in Calipatria State Prison on 21 September 2002, apparently from a heart attack.

TAINTED LOVE

Only one personality type is more disturbing and incomprehensible than a multiple murderer and that is the serial killer 'groupie'. Some of them are deluded women who have convinced themselves that they can redeem a tortured soul through love while others, their even more psychotic sisters, share the predator's perverse desires.

Kenneth Bianchi attracted one such admirer, who offered to make the ultimate sacrifice to procure his release. Wannabe writer and actress Veronica Compton struck up a correspondence with Bianchi during his trial by claiming that she needed his opinion on her play *The Mutilated Cutter*, which concerned a female serial killer.

As their strange 'relationship' intensified through prison visits and voluminous letters, Veronica suggested that she could murder a girl in the same manner as the Hillside Strangler and then dump the body in the same area as the most recent killings. That would make it appear that the real killer was still at large, forcing the authorities to declare her lover innocent. She would even be prepared to smuggle a sample of his semen out of the prison and smear it on the victim.

Veronica was arguably certifiable, but she was not a proficient killer. She needed copious amounts of booze and cocaine before she could summon up enough courage to go through with the scheme and even then she bungled it badly. After talking a young woman into driving her back to her motel in Bellingham

she attempted to strangle her with a cord, but the woman fought her off and escaped. Veronica caught a flight back to California before the police arrived, but the cocktail of cocaine and alcohol she had consumed intensified her mental problems, which tipped her over the edge. She became hysterical and was later arrested in connection with a garbled anonymous letter she had sent to the LAPD, in which she claimed that Bianchi was innocent. As proof, the letter drew their attention to the botched murder attempt in Bellingham.

When detectives investigated the motel incident the intended victim gave them a detailed description of her female assailant, which they matched to the hysterical woman at the airport.

Veronica was jailed for attempted murder, but her passion for sex killers was as ardent as ever. She lost interest in Bianchi and turned her attentions to multiple murderer Douglas Clark [see p.194].

During an exchange of Valentine cards he sent her a photograph of a headless corpse as a love token. She returned the gesture by scribbling a note.

'I take out my straight razor and with one quick stroke I slit the veins in the crook of your arm. Your blood spurts out and spits atop my swelled breasts. Then later that night we cuddle in each other's arms before the fireplace and dress each other's wounds with kisses and loving caresses.'

And she wondered why no one

Veronica Compton had an ingenious scheme to get Bianchi off the hook. Luckily, it failed

had wanted to stage her play.

Despite her failure to sabotage Bianchi's trial she offered to testify on his behalf. She told a convoluted story about a conspiracy to implicate Angelo, but it did not make sense. It was evident she was using the opportunity to get publicity for herself. She did not deny she had talked of opening a mortuary in partnership with Clark so that they could have sex with the dead and she was candid about the other perverse pleasures they were planning if he was ever released. Then she was drawn into admitting her part in trying to lay a false trail by strangling the woman in Bellingham. By the end of the session even Kenneth Bianchi must have been grateful to go back behind bars.

MARLENE OLIVE
AND CHARLES RILEY

In the spring of 1975, 16-year-old Marlene Olive was writing love poems to her adoptive parents while she got high on LSD on the campus of Terra Linda High School in Marin County, California. A few months later, she would douse their dead bodies with kerosene and set them alight after her love-struck boyfriend, 19-year-old Charles 'Chuck' Riley, had killed her mother with a claw hammer and shot her father. Marlene's grisly method of disposal led to the killings becoming known locally as 'the barbecue murders'.

It was a case that aroused a considerable amount of controversy because Marlene was tried as a juvenile, so she received a nominal sentence, whereas 'Chuck' was arraigned as an adult and sentenced to death. This was later commuted to life when the California Court of Appeal ruled that the death sentence was unconstitutional.

Riley's lawyer argued that his client was literally under Marlene's spell at the time of the slayings. He was a shy, insecure and impressionable teenager who had been hypnotized by a manipulative and unbalanced girl, who knew that her lover was uncommonly susceptible to suggestion. The court listened to recordings of Riley undergoing hypnosis by several professional therapists to demonstrate how easily he fell under their influence.

'HE WAS LYING'

But chief prosecuting attorney Josh Thomas dismissed this as mere showmanship. 'If I'd had the slightest doubt of Chuck Riley's guilt, I never would have taken the case,' he told a reporter. 'Under hypnosis, a subject talks in the present when recalling accurately. My expert pointed out that in critical testimony, Riley talked only in the past tense; therefore he was lying.'

Others disagreed. Jill Weissich, the daughter of Riley's attorney William Weissich, had the opportunity to study Marlene at close quarters in court. 'Marlene was definitely not your perky blonde cheerleader type. I had a chance to look into her eyes; she could've cast a spell on a lot of men.'

Riley's neighbours and classmates remembered him as a 'nice boy' who took to wearing black and changed for the worst after he came under the influence of 'wicked' and 'awful' Marlene Olive. But Marlene's counsel, Peter Mitchell, saw things differently. 'Both Marlene and Chuck were heavily involved in drugs and bizarre sex, and she fantasized about lots of things, possibly even killing her parents. But Chuck carried it out. He killed them both.'

Mitchell's faith in his client must have

Led astray? Riley was characterized as a 'nice boy' before he met Marlene Olive and got involved in drugs and bizarre sex

evaporated when he learned she had escaped from Ventura School, the low-security youth detention centre outside Los Angeles, only weeks before her release. It appears that she hustled her way to New York, where she worked as a prostitute to pay for her increasingly demanding drug habit.

In 1981 a reporter tracked her down and persuaded her to agree to a face to face meeting with her former lover, then doing time at the San Luis Obispo prison. The contrast between the two was striking. Marlene was ravaged by drug abuse and directionless, whereas Riley had become fit through a rigorous self-imposed exercise scheme and had educated himself to degree level. There was a long awkward silence at first and then Riley started a long monologue about life in jail.

Marlene was shocked at how well he had coped without her, while she had deteriorated. When Riley finally paused and asked her what she was thinking, she had little to say. 'I'm thinking about all that has gone down. I guess we just lost our marbles.'

BAD SEEDS –

GERALD AND CHARLENE GALLEGO

In the weeks before Christmas the residents of Sacramento, California are out and about in the shopping malls and suburbs, rattling their collection tins to raise money for their favourite charities. In December 1980 the money they raised was in aid of a good cause but it was not for the homeless or the poor. It was to pay for the prosecution of a serial rapist and killer. When the county admitted that its diminished budget meant that it might not be able to afford to sustain proceedings against Gerald Armond Gallego, who had been accused of raping and murdering nine young women, the incensed citizens took their anger out on to the streets. They raised a total of $28,000 to ensure Gallego stayed behind bars until the case against him could be proven beyond all reasonable doubt.

CRIMINAL ROOTS

Gallego's attorney argued that his client was suffering from post-traumatic stress disorder as a result of head injuries he had sustained as a child, which had left him brain-damaged. The condition had been compounded by extreme abuse at a tender age. He was therefore not responsible for his actions and he was not able to 'plan, problem-solve, comprehend or make judgements' regarding his own defence.

Whether any of this was true or not, 34-year-old Gerald Gallego had certainly been capable of planning and problem-solving when he had carried out a series of brutal sexual assaults and murders in California over a two-year period. According to Gallego he simply could not help himself because he was 'infected' with bad blood. His family on both his mother's and his father's side had allegedly been professional criminals and he was therefore genetically predisposed to be antisocial. Although this excuse was blatantly nonsensical, it was a

> GALLEGO HAD CARRIED OUT A SERIES OF BRUTAL SEXUAL ASSAULTS AND MURDERS IN CALIFORNIA OVER A TWO-YEAR PERIOD

Charlene had to put up with Gallego's beatings when he failed to satisfy her and she took a lesbian lover

Evil pairing: Gerald and Charlene met at a poker club and life would never quite be the same

matter of record that Gerald had been offending from an early age. He was just six years old when he was caught breaking into a house and 12 years old when he was placed in a young offender's institution for 'lewd acts' with a six-year-old girl.

At the age of 15 he was arrested for armed robbery and on his release in December 1963 he not only continued to reoffend but he also married the first of five wives. All of them were said to have been beaten and abused by the man one of them called her 'Jekyll and Hyde'.

FROM SOUL MATE TO KILLER'S MATE

Then in the autumn of 1977 Gallego met his soul mate at a poker club. She was an equally disturbed and violent person named Charlene Adell Williams, who was herself twice divorced. However, she soon had to put up with Gallego's abuse and beatings whenever he failed to satisfy her sexually – which was frequently. In her frustration she turned to another woman. Gallego went into a violent rage when he caught them sleeping together, but fortunately the girl escaped with her life. She was one of the luckier ones.

The depth of Gallego's depravity can be gleaned from the fact that he 'celebrated' his thirty-second birthday by sodomizing his own daughter. She had allegedly been abused by him since the age of six.

Gallego's conscience was disengaged and his sense of right and wrong was severely impaired, to say the least. There was nothing and no one to prevent him from unleashing his predatory instincts on the real world. Apparently, though, Charlene did not need convincing. She was up for it too. So on 11 September 1978 they cruised the streets of Sacramento in their Dodge van in search of a sex slave. They couldn't believe their luck when they spotted two teenage girls – 17-year-old Rhonda Scheffler and 16-year-old Kippi Vaught – in a shopping centre. It was easier than they could ever have imagined. Charlene enticed the girls into the back of the van by inviting them to smoke pot and Gallego thrust a loaded revolver into their faces as soon as they were inside. He told them that if they screamed he would shoot them right then and there and then he ordered them to lie face down on the floor of the van so he could bind them

> GALLEGO DROVE TO A SECLUDED SPOT WHILE CHARLENE WATCHED OVER THE GIRLS AND THEN HE RAPED THEM AGAIN AND AGAIN. FINALLY, HE SHOT THEM BOTH AT POINT-BLANK RANGE

with adhesive tape. Gallego drove to a secluded spot while Charlene watched over the girls and then he raped them over and over again. After that he drove to another remote area, where he untied them and ordered them outside. Finally, he shot them both at point-blank range.

Charlene and Gerald were married just over two weeks later, on 30 September 1978. But they did not hang around to celebrate their nuptials because the groom's daughter had filed charges against her father, accusing him of incest and unlawful intercourse. They fled to a hotel in Houston, Texas where Gerald signed in as Stephen Robert Feil.

But Gerald could not contain his bloodlust for long so on 24 June 1979 he ordered Charlene to drive to a nearby county fair, where he hoped to find another unwilling victim. Charlene procured not one but two teenage girls – 14-year-old Brenda Lynne Judd and 13-year-old Sandra Kay Colley – by pretending that she needed help to distribute leaflets and was willing to pay for it. But in a terrible repetition of the first killings the girls were driven to a remote spot in the Nevada desert, where they were raped and murdered – only this time Gerald split their skulls with a hammer.

That autumn the couple moved back to Sacramento where Gerald, still using his alias, found a job as a barman. Then on 24 April 1980 the whole horror was repeated for the third time. Two teenage girls – 17-year-old Karen Chipman Twiggs and 17-year-old Stacy Ann Redican – were abducted in broad daylight.

Charlene had procured them by offering them some marijuana. The brutal pair buried them in shallow graves 20 miles from Lovelock, where

Gerald had killed them in a frenzied attack with a hammer. Gerald and Charlene got married for the second time on 1 June 1980, in an effort to legitimize their alias. Six days afterwards, they abducted 21-year-old Linda Aguilar, who was four months pregnant at the time. Linda was hitching on the highway and she assumed that she would be safe with a married couple, but she was raped, beaten with a rock and left for dead. The pathologist who later performed the autopsy concluded that she had been alive when she had been placed in the hastily dug hole and that in her efforts to crawl free she had pulled in the sand that had suffocated her.

FATAL MISTAKE

So far the duo had abducted strangers but on 17 July 1980 Gerald commemorated his 34th birthday by kidnapping a girl he knew. Thirty-four-year-old barmaid Virginia Mochel was forced into the van as she walked home from the tavern where she worked as a barmaid. She was raped and strangled and then her body was left in undergrowth near Clarksburg.

By now the couple were over-confident and ripe for making a fatal mistake. Eight people had been killed and they had not even been questioned once by the police. They had got away with it and it seemed likely that they would continue to do so, but on 2 November Gerald got cocky and careless. He changed their routine by deciding to abduct a young couple in broad daylight and without using Charlene as bait. After striding up to 22-year-old Craig Miller and 21-year-old Mary Sowers in the street he forced them into the vehicle at gunpoint, in full view of their friends.

Their friends had not seen the gun or they would have called the police right away, but they made a note of the vehicle's licence plate. It seemed strange that Craig and Mary should get into a van owned by a man they had never seen before. They thought they knew all of Craig and Mary's friends and it just did not look right. However, they did not act on their suspicions – there might have been a rational explanation. But when the couple did not return after a few hours their friends called the police and gave them the licence number. It was already too late for Craig and Mary. Gerald killed Craig before taking Mary back to his apartment, where he raped her while Charlene looked on. She was pregnant at the time and unable or unwilling to have sex with her husband, so she did not object to him satiating his lust with another woman. The couple then drove the girl to a lonely spot where Gerald shot her three times.

EVADING EXECUTION

When the police arrived at the couple's apartment they made a cursory search of their vehicle. They quickly found several spent bullet casings, a few reels of duct tape and some restraints, which gave them sufficient grounds to arrest the Gallegos and impound the van.

Charlene did not stand by her man but gave him up on the advice of her attorney, who struck a plea bargain for her. She was sentenced to 16 years and eight months in prison on condition that she would never be extradited to answer charges in any other state. Charlene's testimony secured Gerald's conviction for the murder of Mary Sowers and Craig Miller, for which he was sentenced to death in June 1983. In June of the following year he received

No chance: the Gallegos' bail request is turned down by a court in Sacramento, 1981

a second death sentence for the killing of Karen Twiggs and Stacy Redican, but that sentence was to be ruled invalid 14 years afterwards. The judge had apparently prejudiced the jury by telling them that Gallego might eventually be paroled if he escaped execution.

In March 1999 Gerald instructed his lawyers to appeal against the remaining death sentence on the grounds of insanity. He began to exhibit erratic behaviour such as sleeping under a table in his cell and complaining that people from the 'dark side' were after him.

While Gallego continues to draw out the appeals process in a desperate attempt to impede the wheels of justice, the citizens of Sacramento are satisfied that they contributed in some small way to his incarceration. Ask any one of them and they will tell you that it was money well spent.

KILLING FOR KICKS –
DOUGLAS CLARK AND CAROL BUNDY

At 1 am on the morning of 27 June 1980 Los Angeles resident Jonathan Caravello was hoping he might have stumbled upon something valuable in the alley near his apartment. It was a large stained pine treasure chest with brass decorations and a metal clasp. Prising it open he was almost overcome by a strong nauseating smell and a sight that would haunt him

To compensate for her dowdy appearance, Bundy threw herself at anyone she could find

for the rest of his life. It was a severed human head, partially wrapped in a pair of stained blue jeans and a T-shirt. This was no movie prop. It was the real thing. When the police arrived they took the discovery in their stride. They had been searching for the head for four days after a decapitated corpse had been discovered eight blocks away at the rear of a Studio Sizzler restaurant on Ventura Boulevard. This was a match.

The head was that of a brunette and the wounds matched those on the body that had been found, which had been identified as that of 20-year-old prostitute Exxie Wilson. A cursory examination revealed that the head had been frozen to preserve it and then washed, indicating that the killer had kept it as a trophy.

A more thorough examination back at the morgue produced a copper-jacketed .25 calibre bullet of the same type that had been used in earlier slayings – those of two young stepsisters and a fourth murder victim, 24-year-old prostitute Karen Jones, who had been found on Franklin Avenue. Jones and Wilson were both from Little Rock, Arkansas and their bodies had been found only three miles apart and in the same vicinity as the stepsisters.

At first a pimp known as Albright was named as

A boiler operator in a soap factory, Clark had been fired from a power station for his frequent absences and threats of violence

the chief suspect, but he was swiftly eliminated.

On 12 June the bodies of the teenage stepsisters, Gina Marano and Cynthia Chandler, had been discovered on the sloping embankment along Forest Lawn Drive, near the Ventura Freeway. It was the opposite side of the road to where the 'Hillside Stranglers', Kenneth Bianchi and Angelo Buono, had dumped the body of Yolanda Washington in 1977. The corpse of Laura Collins had been left at the same location in the same year by an unidentified killer.

So the problem facing the Los Angeles Police

Department was that at any one time the 'City of Angels' was the hunting ground for several serial killers, any one of whom could have committed these particular murders. In fact, several spots in and around the city had become dumping grounds for bodies, which only confounded the detectives and gave them the impression that they would have more luck looking for a snake in a jungle.

Then on 30 June the mummified remains of a fifth girl's body were found north of the Golden State Freeway in the San Fernando Valley. From the state of the body the medical examiner was

From suburbs to city centre, Los Angeles has long had an appalling homicide rate, with regular contributions from serial killers

almost certain that this was the first of five linked victims, all of whom had been shot several times with a small calibre pistol, probably a Raven automatic. The girl was later identified as 17-year-old Marnette Comer (also known as Annette Davis), a runaway from Sacramento.

THE SUNSET STRIP KILLERS

When the media heard this story they immediately dubbed the perpetrators the 'Sunset Strip Killers'. Encouraged by the police, who hoped someone would recognize the items, they eagerly publicized the discovery of the pine treasure chest, the jeans and the T-shirt. The jeans were standard issue but

the T-shirt bore the motif 'Daddy's Girl', making it more distinctive, while the chest had been made in Mexico and imported by Chicago Arts, who were able to provide a list of retailers in Los Angeles.

And then, just as the investigation appeared to be gathering momentum, a gruesome discovery threw another variable into the equation. On 9 August the decapitated body of a man was discovered locked in his own van. He had been dead for about five days and was in an advanced state of decomposition due to the stifling heat, but it was evident that the body had been mutilated. Chunks of flesh had been sliced from the buttocks and the torso had been slashed nine times.

Medical Center had called the police after she had admitted to them that she was the murderer of John Murray. During the interview she told the startled officers that she had information that would lead to the arrest of the Sunset Strip Killers. The man responsible for the five murders was her boyfriend, Douglas Clark, she said. She handed them proof in the form of pairs of panties that had belonged to three of the victims. He had kept these items at the home Bundy and he shared in Burbank.

Shortly afterwards one of Clark's colleagues handed in two .25 calibre Raven automatic pistols which Clark had hidden in the boiler room at the Jergens Corporation where he worked. Ballistics matched these to the empty shell casings recovered from the murder scenes, including two from the van in which Murray's body had been found. Clark was clearly implicated in that murder too, despite Bundy's claim to have dispatched the victim herself. Autopsies on both of the decapitated corpses concluded that the knife used in each case was different and the force employed indicated that there had been two different perpetrators.

As the investigation unfolded it was revealed that 37-year-old bespectacled, overweight and

Even without the head he was soon identified as John 'Jack' Robert Murray, a middle-aged part-time country singer from Van Nuys. There appeared to be no connection with the Sunset Strip killings, but on 11 August detectives heard a confession by a nurse, Carol Bundy. Her co-workers at the Valley

IT WAS EVIDENT THE BODY HAD BEEN MUTILATED. CHUNKS OF FLESH HAD BEEN SLICED FROM THE BUTTOCKS AND THE TORSO HAD BEEN SLASHED NINE TIMES

unattractive Bundy had a pathological compulsion to seek affection and acceptance from both men and women to compensate for her dowdy appearance. She had been married three times and was the mother of two young boys. She justified her promiscuity and homicidal rages by claiming that she had been the victim of sexual abuse and that her mother had been violent and unpredictable.

Bundy had been having an affair with John Murray, who was her landlord at the time, but he refused to leave his wife and children, so in December 1979 she threw herself at slim and handsome hustler Douglas Clark, who she met in the bar where Murray was playing. However, Clark was not romantically interested in the middle-aged overweight woman with the thick black glasses. He feigned interest because he saw her as a meal ticket, someone he could squeeze dry until her savings had been spent – and then he would move on to the next sucker. Thirty-one-year-old Clark was the product of a privileged upbringing and he had no difficulty in forming relationships with women of his own age. But he got a kick out of manipulating and exploiting emotionally dependent women and he freely admitted that he was too lazy to work for a living.

SHARED FANTASIES

Clark gave the impression of being a sensitive lover who quoted poetry, but he was secretly obsessed with sick, sadistic fantasies which drove him to torture, necrophilia and murder. Bundy was not faking when she told him that she shared his fantasies. It was not simply a ploy to hold him. And she would prove it by becoming a willing and enthusiastic partner if he wanted to practise them for real. She eagerly consented to sharing him with other women in three-in-a-bed romps and thought nothing of procuring an 11-year-old girl for him or taking indecent photos of the child in pornographic poses with her lover.

So when Clark asked Bundy if she would be willing to kill for him she agreed. She proved it by purchasing two .25 calibre Raven automatics, which she registered in her own name. In April 1980 he returned home with blood on his clothes, but he had a plausible reason. She accepted his explanation until she discovered a bag of blood-stained female garments in his car. Then she

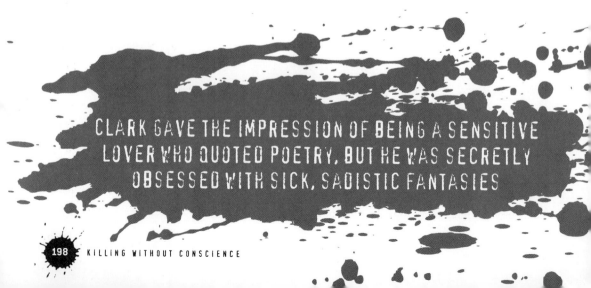

CLARK GAVE THE IMPRESSION OF BEING A SENSITIVE LOVER WHO QUOTED POETRY, BUT HE WAS SECRETLY OBSESSED WITH SICK, SADISTIC FANTASIES

Clark had a ready excuse for the blood on his clothes, but Bundy discovered a bag of bloodstained female garments in his car

demanded that he tell her the truth. The clothes apparently belonged to the murdered stepsisters whose killing was now in the news. One writer has suggested that Bundy was an accomplice in this double killing, that it might have been a test to see how far Clark could trust her, but there is no firm evidence to support this.

By this time Clark had let her know that he was tiring of her and that he expected something to hold his interest — but he was a necrophile, which is a perversion he would be expected to indulge in alone. Clark later confessed that he had offered the two girls a ride when he had seen them waiting at a bus stop on Sunset Strip and that he had shot them in the car when they refused to have sex with him. Then he had raped the lifeless bodies in a rented garage, posing them before disposing of them near Forest Lawn Cemetery. He made no mention of Bundy being present.

It is more likely that Clark confessed to Bundy after she discovered the bag of bloody clothes and that she promised to keep his secret. She saw his confession as a form of intimacy, a way in which she could be indispensable to him. He continued to feed her needs by describing other killings, including the murder of Marnette Comer whose panties he had kept as a trophy. Bundy must have had second thoughts, however, because on 14 June she made an anonymous call to the Van Nuys police department to inform them that her boyfriend was responsible for the murders. But when the switchboard cut her short she did not bother to call back. Either she had been interrupted by Clark or she had realized that she was technically an accessory to murder.

FUN WITH A SEVERED HEAD

On 20 June the pair picked up a hooker in Hollywood's red light district. Both were armed. Bundy was psyched up to shoot the woman as she performed fellatio on Clark, but he lost his temper for some reason and shot the girl himself. They discarded the body at the Magic Mountain amusement park, then went cruising for a second victim in their blue Buick station wagon. Clark was not satisfied that the night had lived up to his expectations so he left Bundy at home and picked up Exxie Wilson on the Sunset Strip, where he paid her to perform oral sex. Then he shot her and cut off her head. It was still in a bag on the back seat when he returned to the corner where he had seen Exxie touting for business with a blonde. Karen Jones recognized him and did not hesitate to climb into his car. Then he shot her too and dropped her

When the severed head of Exxie Wilson lost its lustre, they cleaned it up and placed it in the treasure chest for disposal

body behind the Burbank Studios.

The couple kept the severed head in the freezer for sick games, which Carol later described as casually as if she was recalling watching the Los Angeles Dodgers.

'Where I had my fun was with the make-up. I was making her over like a big Barbie doll.'

Clark then performed oral sex on the head and played with it in the shower. But after three days the head had lost its lustre so they cleaned it up and placed it in the treasure chest for disposal. Crazy they might have been but Carol kept her wits about her, using gloves to make sure she did not leave any fingerprints.

On 1 August Clark told Bundy that earlier that day he had taken his neighbour's 11-year-old daughter for a drive. She was a witness to him picking up a hooker, who he shot and afterwards had sex with before dumping the body in Antelope Valley.

Four days later Bundy sounded out John

Murray. She wanted to see how he would react to hearing of her participation in a series of unsolved murders, but he was unimpressed. In fact, he threatened to go to the police – so she killed him on the spot and then cut off his head. But in her excitement she neglected to recover the shell casings. And then she remembered that there had been a witness. Clark's latest conquest had seen Bundy with Murray that morning and she would have no hesitation in informing the police in order to get Bundy out of the way.

CONFLICTING STATEMENTS

It was the realization that Clark would be free while she languished in prison that led to Bundy's breakdown and confession, though she attempted to blame him for corrupting her. He countered by claiming that she had committed all of the murders without his knowledge or participation. Their conflicting statements were a classic case of denial and projection as they attempted to rewrite their past, with the other cast in the role of the killer and themselves as the reluctant accomplice. Clark had initially attempted to implicate John Murray, but detectives quickly proved that the dead man had been seen elsewhere at the time of the killings.

In the end the forensic evidence damned them both. Clark's fingerprints were found on one of the two guns although he had insisted that they both belonged to Bundy. Clark had also left a bloody footprint in the rented garage and blood stains in a car. He had sold the car to keep it out of the hands of the police. Detectives also recovered the gloves that Bundy had worn when packing Exxie Wilson's head, together with a recording of Clark's confession. A witness identified his voice as that of the man who had telephoned her to confess to the killing of Cynthia Chandler. He had called her twice, so she was certain it was the same man.

On the first occasion he had claimed to be a police officer investigating the case and on the second he told her that he had killed Chandler and he would kill her too.

After they were charged, Bundy and Clark were subjected to stringent psychological assessments which concluded that they had no physical impairments or disorders that would excuse or explain their behaviour. They were both pathological liars and had indulged in

THE COUPLE KEPT THE SEVERED HEAD IN THE FREEZER FOR SICK GAMES, WHICH CAROL LATER DESCRIBED AS CASUALLY AS IF RECALLING WATCHING THE LA DODGERS

abnormal sexual behaviour, but they were mentally fit to stand trial.

SEND ME TO THE GAS CHAMBER

The trial, which Deputy District Attorney Robert Jorgensen described as 'an intimate tour of a sewer', ran for four months from October 1982. Clark was charged with killing six women. He was believed to have killed seven, but the bullet found in the seventh victim was too damaged for ballistics to identify it. On the stand Bundy testified that Clark had boasted of killing 47 women and of having begun his criminal career at the age of 17, but that sounded like an empty and vulgar boast to the jury who could only return a verdict based on the facts.

Clark attempted to defend himself, but his frequent tantrums and abusive outbursts, and the admission that he was an unrepentant necrophiliac, did nothing to convince the jury that he was innocent. After he had insulted the judge, whom he called a 'gutless worm', his attorneys were ordered to take over. On 28 January 1983, after five days' deliberation, the jurors agreed on a guilty verdict which prompted Clark to demand that the judge sentence him to die in the gas chamber. On 15 February he got his wish in spades. The judge handed down six death sentences, one for each of his victims.

CHANGE OF PLEA

On 2 May 1983, just before her trial was about to begin, Carol Bundy changed her plea to guilty in a deal that saved the state a long and expensive trial and took the death penalty off the table.

In return she received two consecutive life sentences for her crimes. She claimed that she was finished with her two-timing ex-lover, but she continued to write to him, even offering to hang herself if he asked her to.

But Douglas Clark had forged a new relationship with a woman who had been accused of attempted murder. Serial killer groupie Veronica Compton [see page 185] had earlier developed an infatuation with serial killer Kenneth Bianchi and had been prepared to murder a woman in a copy-cat killing in order to cast doubt on his conviction. It seemed that Clark had finally found his soul mate. He wrote to her thanking her for sex in a prison visiting room and calling his love rival, Bianchi, a 'whiney bitch'.

CLARK BOASTED OF KILLING 47 WOMEN AFTER BEGINNING HIS CRIMINAL CAREER AT 17, BUT THAT SOUNDED LIKE A VULGAR BOAST TO THE JURY

THE COLUMBINE KILLINGS –
ERIC HARRIS AND DYLAN KLEBOLD

These days we are no longer shocked to hear of incidents of road rage, air rage or even supermarket rage as tempers flare and violence erupts in places that we once thought were safe. But though we are becoming increasingly indifferent to such events, it is still horrifying to hear of a school shooting because this breaks the last taboo. Even the roughest inner city institutions should be a place where our children can be safe. The fear that their child might be the victim of a shooting by a classmate, or that their own child might be capable of killing, is something no parent can ever come to terms with.

NO WARNING

The massacre at Columbine High School near Denver on 20 April 1999 has been blamed in part on the parents of the two teenage boys who killed 12 pupils and a teacher and wounded 24 other people before turning the guns on themselves. But investigators have admitted that the parents of Eric David Harris and Dylan Bennet Klebold had no idea of their sons' state of mind, or of their plans. Neither boy was neglected, abused, bullied or encouraged to worship weapons, nor were they obsessed with violent video games, heavy metal or movies as the media have suggested. And

Self-centred sociopaths: Klebold (above) and Harris

contrary to what has been suggested by various anti-Semitic websites, they were not anti-Christian avengers or white supremacists.

The unpalatable truth is that Harris and Klebold were all-American teenagers who could not take the rejection that is a normal part of growing up. Had they been born in a country where automatic weapons are not sold over the counter to anyone who can afford them, they might have taken out their rage by vandalizing the school or beating up the kids they did not like.

But contrary to the version of events marketed by the sensation-seeking media, the boys did not compile a list of enemies. Their initial plan was to set off dozens of home-made bombs in the campus cafeteria and kitchen, which would demolish the school and kill hundreds of students, friends and enemies alike, in a random act that would symbolize their rage and despair.

They had also planted more devices in their cars, which they had parked at strategic points to wreak the maximum havoc. Their intention was to watch the ensuing chaos from outside and then when the police and concerned parents arrived they were going to detonate the car bombs too. It was the ultimate revenge fantasy. They believed that the institution and the people in it were responsible for their isolation and unpopularity. It was only after the bombs had failed to explode that the boys went on the rampage.

Harris and Klebold had been building up their resentment for years – they had even boasted about it to the few friends they had. But when their plans were laughed at they had to carry out their threat or lose face. For two deeply disturbed and suicidal teenagers losing face was a fate worse than death. So they chose to die and bring down everything they hated along with them. They were not ordinary kids who had been corrupted by playing Black Sabbath records backwards but embittered, self-centred sociopaths. Klebold was a paranoid depressive who described himself as 'a god of sadness', while Harris suffered from the same narcissistic paranoia that drove dictators Adolf Hitler and Saddam Hussein.

'I feel like God and I wish I was, having everyone being OFFICIALLY lower than me,' he once wrote.

The two complemented one another and together they found the will to inflict their punishment on a world that had rejected them – or so they imagined. No one saw the danger signs because they were two white kids from

KLEBOLD WAS A PARANOID DEPRESSIVE WHO DESCRIBED HIMSELF AS 'A GOD OF SADNESS', WHILE HARRIS SUFFERED FROM NARCISSISTIC PARANOIA

Harris and Klebold had nurtured their resentment for years, dreaming of making the world pay attention to them

affluent American families. And being devious and intelligent they had managed to mitigate the fears of everyone who had expressed concern simply by telling them what they wanted to hear. They had learned to lie convincingly and conceal their true feelings – except in their journals and video diaries, to which they confided every perceived injustice they had suffered. This is one of the last entries Harris wrote.

'I hate you people for leaving me out of so many fun things. And no don't say, "Well, that's your fault," because it isn't, you people had my phone number, and I asked and all, but no. No no no don't let the weird-looking Eric KID come along.'

His exercise books were said to be covered in swastikas.

Klebold was more introspective and he was consumed by despair. He confided to his diary that his life was 'the most miserable existence in the history of time'. He drew hearts in his journals and considered himself misunderstood and victimized by fate.

Both teenagers loathed authority and despised anyone who made the effort to fit in and conform. Their attack was not spontaneous because it had been germinating for months. They had even taken after school jobs to pay for the weapons and the bomb-making ingredients. If Harris and Klebold had been able to raise more money to buy more guns, and had taken more care to build better bombs, the fatalities might have been counted in triple figures.

INDEX

ACKNOWLEDGEMENTS AND PICTURE CREDITS

The author gratefully acknowledges the following as primary sources of background material for this book.

The Sacramento Bee, January 2000
http://www.crimezzz.net
http://www.truetv.com

Picture Credits

Shutterstock: Page 8, 15, 16, 22, 44, 45, 50, 54, 58, 66, 67, 70, 71, 74, 81, 86, 89, 92, 93, 96, 98, 102, 104, 112, 118, 119, 130, 133, 134, 135, 138, 140, 144, 146, 154, 158, 160, 164, 168, 172, 175, 177, 181, 190, 196, 199, 200

corbis: 25, 29, 30, 33, 37, 38, 41 (2), 42, 46, 49, 77, 78, 85, 91, 101, 108, 115, 163, 171 (2), 184, 203 (2), 205

rex: 117 (2), 123 (2), 124, 129 (2), 153 (2), 157 (b), 161, 189, 193

topfoto: 11, 13, 57 (2), 61, 107, 183, 195

Mary Evans: 19

Riverside Public Library: 21 (2)

Peter Gray: 63, 80, 83, 148, 151, 185, 187, 194

ZUMA Press: 65 (top: Clay Miller); 65 (bottom: P. Kuroda)

Serial Killers TV: 69

PA: 73 (2), 137, 141, 142, 149, 167 (2)

Nova Scotia Archives and Records Management: 53

getty: 105, 147, 165

AAP: 157 (t)